Addressing the Weaknesses of Multi-Criteria Decision-
Making Methods using Python

T0293054

Semra Erpolat Taşabat /
Tuğba Kıral Özkan / Olgun Aydın

Addressing the Weaknesses of Multi-Criteria Decision-Making Methods using Python

PETER LANG

Berlin - Bruxelles - Chennai - Lausanne - New York - Oxford

Library of Congress Cataloging-in-Publication Data
A CIP catalog record for this book has been applied for at the
Library of Congress.

Bibliographic information published by the Deutsche Nationalbibliothek.
The German National Library lists this publication in the German National
Bibliography; detailed bibliographic data is available on the Internet at
http://dnb.d-nb.de.

Cover illustration: © Dmitry Demidovich / shutterstock.com

ISBN 978-3-631-91334-5 (Print)
E-ISBN 978-3-631-91337-6 (E-PDF)
E-ISBN 978-3-631-92341-2 (EPUB)
DOI 10.3726/b22103

© 2024 Peter Lang Group AG, Lausanne

Published by Peter Lang GmbH, Berlin, Deutschland
info@peterlang.com - www.peterlang.com

This publication has been peer reviewed.

Preface

We are pleased to present the book titled "Addressing the Weaknesses of Multi-Criteria Decision-Making Methods Using Python". The book aims to provide insights into the weaknesses of Multi-Criteria Decision-Making (MCDM) methods used in various aspects of decision-making and to enhance the accuracy and effectiveness of MCDM methods in selecting the best alternatives in various domains. The book is divided into four chapters, each of which provides a comprehensive overview of the subject matter. The first chapter provides general information about decision-making and MCDM, setting the foundation for understanding the concepts and principles behind MCDM methods. The second chapter elaborates on the most used and basic MCDM methods, discussing how to compute the measurement value, decide on a weighting strategy, reduce the decision matrix to a single unit, and sort the outcomes using these methods. The third chapter focuses on the weaknesses of MCDM methods and provides a detailed analysis of how these weaknesses can impact the outcomes of MCDM methods. The final chapter introduces modified methods that aim to overcome the weaknesses identified in the previous sections. These new methods are developed based on the insights gained from analyzing the weaknesses of existing MCDM methods. The Inequality-adjusted Human Development Index (IHDI) data will be used to demonstrate the working of both traditional and modified versions of them. We hope that this book will be a valuable resource for professionals in various fields interested in MCDM and its applications.

Table of Contents

List of Abbreviations

AHP :	Analytic Hierarchy Process
ELECTRE :	ELimination Et Choix Traduisant la REalite´- ELimination and Choice Expressing the Reality
HDI :	Human Development Index
IHDI :	Inequality-adjusted Human Development Index
HDRO :	Human Development Report Office
MADM :	Multi Attribute Decision-Making
MAUT :	Multi Attribute Utility Theory
MCDA :	Multi-Criteria Decision Analysis
MCDM :	Multi-Criteria Decision-Making
MODM :	Multi Objective Decision-Making
PROMETHEE :	Preference Ranking Organization Methods for Enrichment Evaluation
TOPSIS :	Technique for Order Preference by Similarity to an Ideal Solution
VIKOR :	VIsekriterijumska optimizacija i KOmpromisno Resenje

List of Figures

List of Tables

Introduction

The book titled "Addressing the Weaknesses of Multi-Criteria Decision-Making Methods Using Python" aims to address the weaknesses of Multi-Criteria Decision-Making (MCDM) methods used in various aspects of decision-making. The book is divided into four chapters.

Chapter 1: Decision-Making and Multi-Criteria Decision-Making (Introduction): The first part of the book provides general information about decision-making and MCDM. It sets the foundation for understanding the concepts and principles behind MCDM methods.

Chapter 2: Some of The Most Popular MCDM Methods: The second section elaborates on the most commonly used and basic MCDM methods. It discusses how to compute the measurement value, decide on a weighting strategy, reduce the decision matrix to a single unit, and sort the outcomes using these methods. The book makes clear that any MCDM method can provide different outcomes if at least one of these weaknesses is used.

Chapter 3: Weaknesses of MCDM Methods: The third section of the book focuses on the weaknesses mentioned in the previous section. It provides a detailed analysis of how these weaknesses can impact the outcomes of MCDM methods. The book emphasizes the importance of recognizing and addressing these weaknesses to improve decision-making processes.

Chapter 4: Investigation of The Weaknesses of MCDM Methods: In the final section, the book introduces modified methods that aim to overcome the weaknesses identified in the previous sections. These new methods are developed based on the insights gained from analyzing the weaknesses of existing MCDM methods. The Inequality-adjusted Human Development Index (IHDI) data will be used to demonstrate the working of both traditional and modified versions of them.

The book aims to draw attention to the weaknesses in MCDM methods and provide insights into improving decision-making processes. By addressing these weaknesses, it seeks to enhance the accuracy and effectiveness of MCDM methods in selecting the best alternatives in various domains.

Chapter 1   Decision-Making and Multi-Criteria Decision-Making

In this section, we are going to provide insight and details into the decision-making process and then we are going to handle this process from a multi-criteria perspective.

1.1. Decision-Making

Decision-making is the process of selecting the most appropriate option from a range of choices to achieve specific objectives set by the decision makers.

It is a multi-step process we engage in regularly. According to (Simon, 1977), managerial decision-making aligns with the broader managerial process, which encompasses functions like planning, organizing, and controlling. These functions involve addressing questions such as what needs to be done, when, where, and by whom (Sharda, Delen, & Turban, 2013).

While the number of steps may vary depending on the source, the core stages typically include "defining, identifying, and development". Additional steps can be incorporated to expand the process when necessary.

The decision-making process is complex and involves input from various managers or individuals, as well as the use of data, information, and technology. The shared objective among all participants is undoubtedly to identify the best possible alternative for decision makers, considering the perspectives of everyone involved.

The decision-making process was depicted through a diverse array of models, created by several experts. The most renowned model is the one introduced by Herber T.A. Simon, a Nobel Prize Laureate and a management researcher at Carnegie-Mellon University.

Simon (1977) proposed a systematic decision-making process consisting of three major phases: Intelligence, Design, and Choice. He later added a fourth phase, Implementation, and Monitoring as a fifth phase for feedback.

Simon's model, referred to as Simon's Theory of Decision-Making Process, is largely acknowledged as the most succinct and comprehensive representation of rational decision-making. Figure 1.1 in Delen's

(Delen, 2020, s. 21).work displays a conceptual representation of the decision-making process as proposed by Simon. This diagram is found on next page

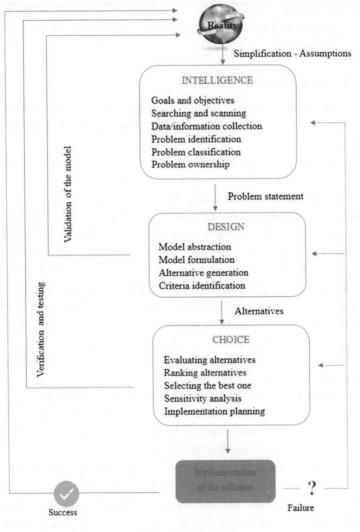

Figure 1.1: Simon's four steps of the decision-making.

1.1.1. Phase 1: Intelligence

The intelligence phase involves periodic or ongoing scanning of the environment, which also includes a number of actions meant to identify issues, circumstances, or opportunities. This phase may also include tracking the results of a decision-making process that was already finished at the implementation stage.

Identifying and evaluating corporate goals and objectives is part of the intelligence phase. It entails figuring out whether an issue is present, characterizing it clearly, assessing its severity, and identifying its symptoms. Real-world issues are frequently complicated, making it challenging to discern between symptoms and actual issues. Examining the sources of symptoms may reveal new opportunities and issues. By keeping an eye on and evaluating the productivity level of the organization, one can ascertain whether a problem exists. Real data should serve as the foundation for both model construction and productivity measurement. The most difficult parts of the process are gathering and projecting future data.

1.1.2. Phase 2: Design

The design phase of the decision-making process involves several key activities aimed at understanding the problem and developing feasible solutions.

During the design phase, potential courses of action are identified, developed, and analyzed. These include comprehending the issue and determining the viability of potential remedies. Modeling is the process of abstracting an issue into a quantitative or qualitative form. The variables are determined for a mathematical model, along with their interrelationships. Because of the cost-benefit trade-off, an appropriate balance between the degree of model simplification and the depiction of reality must be achieved. A more straightforward model is less representational of the actual issue and may yield unreliable conclusions, but it is simpler, easier to manipulate, and faster to solve. In addition, a simpler model usually uses less data, or the data is easier to get and aggregated. Modeling is a process that combines science and art. As with any art, valid solutions require ingenuity and dexterity in figuring out what simplifying assumptions may be used, how to combine suitable properties of the model classes, and how to integrate models to get valid solutions. A principle of choice is a standard that characterizes whether a solution approach is acceptable. It is an outcome variable in a model. Choosing a choice principle includes how someone sets goals for decision-making and integrates those goals into models; it is not a part of the choosing phase. We may want to take a low-risk approach or a large risk. We may also try to achieve satisfice or optimization. Understanding the distinction between a constraint and a criterion is also crucial. While a criterion aids in ranking and choosing the best viable solution, restrictions aid in defining the feasible solution space.

1.1.3. Phase 3: Choice

A crucial stage in the decision-making process is the choosing phase, during which a choice and commitment to pursue a certain course of action are formed. Since decision-makers might work in both phases and switch back and forth between design and choice activities frequently, it can be difficult to draw a distinct line between them. During the choosing phase, a model's suitable solution a particular collection of values for the decision variables in a chosen alternative is found, assessed, and recommended. Finding the best course of action requires applying analytical methods, algorithms, heuristics, and blind searches while solving a decision-making model. Every option needs to be assessed, and if it has several objectives, each needs to be looked at and weighed against the others. What-if analysis investigates significant changes in parameters, whereas sensitivity analysis assesses how robust a certain option is. Managers can identify the values of decision variables to achieve a particular goal by using goal-seeking.

The steps taken during the choice phase are summarized as follows:

- Solution to the model
- Sensitivity analysis
- Selection of the best alternative(s)
- Plan for implementation

The distinction between the design and choice phases is unclear because some tasks can be completed in either phase, and the decision-maker can move from choice to design tasks by coming up with new options while assessing the ones already available.

1.1.4. Phase 4: Implementation

A new order of things or a change is essentially introduced when a suggested solution to a problem is put into practice. Change also has to be controlled. Change management requires the management of user expectations. Because implementation is a protracted, intricate process with ill-defined limits, the term is fairly difficult to define. In essence, the step of implementation is putting a suggested solution into practice, rather than simply putting in place a computer system.

Based on SIMON's model, a series of alternative models and methods were developed for decision-making. Below is a list of the most well-known models and methods (Brândaş, 2007):

Paterson's process of decision-making (Hoven, 1996)

- Kotter's process model (Dearden, 1983)
- Pounds' Flowchart of managerial behavior (Pounds, 1969)
- Kepner-Tregoe's method (Kepner & Tregoe, 1965)
- Hammond's model (Hammond, Keeney, & Raiffa, 1999)
- Couger's model (Couger, 1995, 1996)
- Pokras' methodology (Pokras, 1989)
- Harrison's models (Peters, 1999)

There are also numerous perspectives on the decision-making process in the literature, some of which include Peters (1999), Jett and George (2005), Nooraie (2008), Wildman and Salas (2009), Nobrega, O'Hara, Sadasivuni and Dumas (2009), Verboncu (2011), Jalal-Karim (2013), Negulescu (2014).

The act of making a decision involves a decision problem, which the decision-maker must comprehend and precisely define in order to come up with solutions. A number of obstacles have been found in the way of a precise definition of the problem under consideration: focusing on effects rather than causes, selective perception, outlining issues with potential solutions, etc. (Cornescu, Marinescu, Curteanu, & Toma, 1999).

Simple models of decision-making process consist of steps to follow that guide participants in decision-making. The stages or steps of the decision-making process may show differences based on the researcher's approach.

1.2. Classification of Decision-Making

1.2.1. According to the Amount of Information Possessed

Decision-making may be classified under one of these categories below:

1. Decision-making under certainty.
2. Decision-making under risk.
3. Decision-making under uncertainty.
4. Decision-making under partial information.
5. Decision-making in competitive situations.

1.2.1.1. Decision-Making Under Certainty

Decision-making under certainty refers to circumstances in which we know exactly under what circumstances solutions will be implemented. This type of decision-making is deterministic in nature and assumes that all necessary information is available to the decision-maker.

Certainty means that the decision maker has all the necessary information he or she needs. Therefore, the decision-maker can choose the most beneficial alternative among other alternatives, knowing the possible results.

Linear programming models and Analytical hierarchical processes are the models that can be used for decision-making with certainty (Taha, 2007).

1.2.1.2. Decision-Making Under Risk

In decision-making under risk, also known as scholastic decision-making, different numbers of conditions are in question, and the results that each strategy achieves under each condition are achieved within a specific probability framework. It is a strategy applied in the stage of expected value solution.

Probability distributions describe the payoffs associated with each decision alternative under risky conditions. For this reason, choosing decisions when facing risk can be based on the expected value criterion, which compares decision alternatives by maximizing expected profit or minimizing expected cost (Taha, 2007).

1.2.1.3. Decision-Making Under Uncertainty

Uncertainty is known as the situation in which information about alternatives is insufficient or inadequate and future events are impossible to predict. It means that the decision maker makes a decision without being knowledgeable about the outcomes of the alternatives. In general, uncertainty often stems from factors such as the unpredictability of significant events or outcomes and a shortage of available data. It can be observed in various domains, including the business literature, where uncertainties relate to technological, social, environmental, or financial factors, climate modeling, where uncertainties arise in estimating greenhouse gas emissions and concentrations, the field of robotics, where challenges include sensor imprecision and unreliable communication channels, and decision support systems, where uncertainty pertains to predicting how a human operator will respond (Badings, Sim~ao, Suilen, & Jansen, 2023).

Uncertainty is known as the situation in which information about alternatives is insufficient or inadequate and future events are impossible to predict. It means that the decision maker makes a decision without being knowledgeable about the outcomes of the alternatives. Since 1957, the fundamental concept of strict uncertainty in decision-making has remained largely unchanged. When the work of pound and Raiffa (1957) is compared to French's handbook (1989), it is found that both sources cover similar topics regarding the foundational principles, characteristics, and criteria for decision-making under strict uncertainty. The commonly recognized criteria include Laplace (1985), Wald's maximin (1949), Hurwicz's (1951), and Savage's (1951). Remarkably, there have been no new criteria introduced since then. These can be summarized as follows (Ballestero, 2002). In such situations, the decision-making criteria and explanations are given below:

1.2.1.3.1. The Criterion of Optimism (Maximax)

The Maximax criterion represents an optimistic approach to decision-making. It advises the decision maker to assess the maximum potential outcomes of various alternatives and select the one with the best outcome. This criterion is particularly attractive to adventurous decision-makers who are drawn to the prospect of high rewards. It may also resonate with individuals who are willing to take risks and can handle potential losses without significant inconvenience. The Maximax decision rule is particularly suitable for modeling individuals with an optimistic profile, especially when the payoffs are positive-flow rewards like profits or revenue. However, when payoffs are presented as negative-flow rewards such as costs, the optimist's decision rule becomes the minimin. It's important to note that negative-flow rewards are expressed as positive numbers. To follow the Maximax decision rule: Evaluate the maximum payoff achievable for each action alternative (corresponding to matrix rows). Among these maximum values, select the option with the highest payoff. This chosen action alternative represents the decision (Pažek & Rozman, 2009).

1.2.1.3.2. The Criterion of Pessimism (Maximin)

Wald's Maximin Criterion, introduced in 1950, can be seen as a strategy employed in situations of complete ignorance. It is a strategy that effectively responds to nature's minimax strategy. Even in cases of total uncertainty, Wald's criterion is notably cautious, and while this level of conservatism may appear excessive, it can be justifiable in certain circumstances, as noted by Wen and Iwamura (2008) (Pažek & Rozman, 2009). This criterion represents a pessimistic approach to decision-making and focuses on the safety aspect of each decision, specifically, the worst possible outcome associated with each choice. It differs from Laplace's criterion, proposed in 1825, which doesn't emphasize security as much. In simpler terms, Wald seeks to determine the minimum potential benefit corresponding to the least favorable consequence for each decision. For instance, when comparing two actions, $a_1 = (15, 23, 9, 46, 12, 4)$ and $a_2 = (36, 15, 21, 3, 14, 15)$, according to Wald's criterion, the decision maker, characterized as an extreme pessimist, assesses the security levels of each action, which are 4 and 3, respectively. Since the first action has a higher security level, it is chosen. However, there are logical and psychological objections to Wald's criterion. To determine the security level for a_1, the decision maker imagines that a_{16} will be the true state of the world, while for a_2, they imagine that a_{24} will be true. This process appears inconsistent. Psychologists argue that most decision makers do not adhere to Wald's maximin criterion, as it tends to exhibit a significant bias towards irrational pessimism (Ballestero, 2002). It is particularly appealing to risk-averse decision makers who value the assurance that, in the event of an unfavorable outcome, there is at least a known minimum payoff. This approach is justifiable because minimum payoffs may have a higher likelihood of occurring, and the lowest possible outcome could result in a highly unfavorable situation (Pažek & Rozman, 2009).

1.2.1.3.3. The Criterion of Realism (Hurwicz)

The Hurwicz criterion, introduced by Leonid Hurwicz in 1951, is one of the most widely recognized decision-making methods. It seeks a balanced approach between extreme optimism and extreme pessimism by considering both perspectives. Instead of adopting an entirely optimistic or pessimistic stance, Hurwicz combines a degree of each by assigning a specific percentage weight to optimism (denoted as "a") and the remainder to pessimism $(1 - a)$. To apply the Hurwicz criterion, a weighted average is computed for each action alternative, with " a " representing the index of pessimism. The action alternative with the highest average is selected. The choice of " a " reflects the decision maker's risk tolerance. A more cautious decision maker will set " a " closer to 1, effectively favoring pessimism and aligning the Hurwicz criterion with the maximin criterion. Conversely, a more adventurous decision maker will set " a " closer to 0 , favoring optimism and aligning the Hurwicz criterion with the maximax criterion (Pažek & Rozman, 2009). However, when decision makers represent collective entities, such as social groups, practicality and relevance of applying the Hurwicz criterion become uncertain. This is due to the inherent challenges, both in terms of logic and practice, in determining the " a " value when dealing with diverse opinions, preferences, and beliefs within groups. According to French (1988), this as a significant weakness of Hurwicz's criterion. Additionally, it's important to note that this decision rule does not meet a critical requirement, which is the use of consistent weight systems, where each state of the world corresponds to one and only one weight (Ballestero, 2002).

1.2.1.3.4. The Criterion of Regret (Savage)

The Savage Minimax Regret criterion is a decision-making approach that focuses on assessing regret, which represents the loss, opportunity cost, or disadvantage incurred when a specific situation arises, and the selected alternative yields a smaller payoff than what could have been achieved in that situation. Regret, in this context, corresponds to a particular payoff X_{ij} and is defined as $R_{ij} = X_j\left(\max\right) - X_{ij}$, where $X_j\left(max\right)$ is the highest attainable payoff under the situation S_j. This definition of regret enables the decision maker to transform the payoff matrix into a regret matrix. The minimax criterion within this framework involves evaluating the maximum regret for each strategy and selecting the strategy with the smallest maximum regret. This approach is appealing to cautious decision makers who aim to ensure that the chosen alternative performs well when compared to other options, regardless of the specific situation that unfolds. It is particularly useful for decision makers who are aware that they will be evaluated against competitors facing similar or identical circumstances. The Minimax Regret criterion places a strong emphasis on avoiding the worst possible consequences when making a decision. While regret is typically an emotional state and challenging to measure accurately due to its subjectivity, the assumption is made that regret is quantifiable and directly related to the rewards R_{ij} expressed in the payoff matrix. This means that a real loss, such as a financial loss, is considered equivalent to a missed opportunity to gain, both of which are treated as regret in this criterion. Regret is the measure of the potential loss that the decision maker may experience if they choose action alternative A_i and state of nature S_j occurs. Opportunity loss (OL) is the discrepancy between the optimal outcome that could have been achieved under S_j and the actual outcome that occurs when A_i is chosen in the presence of S_j. Hence, when the decision alternative achieves the highest potential payoff for a specific state of nature, the opportunity loss is regarded as zero. Any alternative result leads to a favorable missed opportunity, suggesting remorse (Pažek & Rozman, 2009).

1.2.1.3.5. The Criterion of Equal Likelihood (Laplace)

Laplace's criterion (1825) is based on the idea that if there is no available information regarding the probabilities of different outcomes, it is reasonable to assume that they are equally likely. Laplace's argument draws from Jakob Bernoulli's Principle of Insufficient Reason, which suggests that when prior knowledge is lacking, events should be assumed to have equal probability. So, if there are n possible outcomes, each is assigned a probability of 1/n. According to this approach, the decision maker calculates the expected payoff for each alternative and selects the one with the highest expected value. This characteristic distinguishes this approach from criteria that consider only extreme payoffs, making it more akin to decision-making under risk. Laplace asserts that to approach uncertainty rationally, probability theory should be applied. This entails that for each state of nature

(S_j in S), the decision maker should assess the probability $\left(p_j\right)$ of S_j occurring, which can be determined theoretically, empirically, or subjectively (Pažek & Rozman, 2009), (Ballestero, 2002).

1.2.1.4. Decision-Making Under Partial Information

Decisions are made using only this partial knowledge when the probability distribution's shape (normal, poisson, binomial, etc.) is known and information about the distribution's parameters and characteristics (mean, median, skewness, kurtosis, etc.) is available.

An estimated uncertainty model must be used if the precise probability distribution on the set of states is unknown or poorly understood. Now, one may easily continue by using the Bayes-criterion if the extra data is sufficient to estimate a prior probability distribution. The Bayesian approach to decision making necessitates the decision maker (DM) to have comprehensive judgments in terms of preferences, risk attitudes, and beliefs. (Insua, 1992). This means that the numerical inputs (values, utilities, and probabilities) to the analysis must be precise. In order to evaluate these inputs, the DM's judgmental inputs must be encoded into parameters and an evaluation function must be assigned to each option. In actuality, the DM might not be prepared or able to offer the details required to find the parameters with accuracy. Rather, he might just provide a few limitations on his conclusions, such as the need that we operate inside a family of values, probabilities, and utilities. This is at odds with the tenets of Bayesian theory. This decision-making process will be referred to as decision making under partial information (Insua, 1992).

1.2.1.5. Decision-Making in Competitive Situations

In a competitive situation, decision-making is the process of selecting the best course of action in order to achieve a desired outcome, given the actions of other competitors. Competitive decision-making can be complex and challenging, as it requires considering a wide range of factors, including strengths and weaknesses, the strengths and weaknesses of competitors, and the overall market conditions. There are a number of different frameworks and approaches that can be used to make decisions in competitive situations. One common approach is to use game theory, which is a branch of mathematics that studies strategic decision-making. Game theory can be used to model a wide range of competitive situations, from simple two-player games like chess to complex multi-player games like business competitions. Another common approach to decision-making in competitive situations is to use scenario planning. Scenario planning is a process of developing and evaluating alternative plans for the future, based on different possible scenarios. Scenario planning can help to identify and prepare for a range of different possible outcomes, including unexpected events and changes in the competitive landscape (Arend, 2020; Dyson, 2021).

1.2.2. Classification of Decision Types

Decision-making can be classified in various ways according to the structure of the decision problem, its scope, importance, and effect. Gorry and Scott Morton classified decision-making into two groups being the level and type of decision (Gorry & Morton, 1971).

1.2.2.1. Level of Decision

Structured decisions: These decisions are made when the decision process is well-structured. Also known as **programmed decisions**, structured decisions are repetitive and routine daily decisions. In this type of decision, problems are well-defined, certainty level is high, and the decision maker does not have subjective flexibility.

The majority of structured decisions are those that can be automated by computers without the need for a person. A structured decision is one where one can specify the inputs, outputs, and internal procedures connected with the stages of the decision. The term "stage of structured decisions" refers to any decision stage for which the aforementioned standards apply. A methodical approach to making decisions is referred to as a well-structured process.

Semi-structured decisions: Even though some of these judgments are structured in some way, we cannot classify them as structured decisions. This indicates that out of the three stages, only one or two are structured. In this case, computers are of great help because most of the company's fall into this category (Brândaş, 2007).

Non-structured decisions: Decisions that lack a clear explanation of the three stages involved in the decision-making process. One cannot identify any one of the three stages—inputs, outputs, and internal processes—in this scenario. This kind of challenge can arise when a decision that needs to be taken is either really recent or was not thoroughly considered. In this instance, computers can assist users in making these unstructured decisions; the main issue is the amount of labor that humans must accomplish.

1.2.2.2. Type of Decision

The process of choosing the optimal course of action from a range of options is known as decision-making. Decisions can be classified in many ways, one of which is according to their aim. The aim of a decision refers to what the decision-maker intends to achieve by making the decision (Bera, Mahapatra, Mondal, Acharjya, & Koley, 2023).
There are three main types of decisions according to aim:

Strategic decisions: Those decisions that have a long-term impact on the majority of the company or the entire organization. These decisions affect the objectives and strategies of the organizations. Typically, the management of the company makes these choices.

Tactical decisions or control decisions: They have an impact on how an organization's division will carry out its operations in the future. These choices are usually made as part of a larger strategic decision. These decisions are typically made by managers at the middle management level of the organization, which is below those who run the company and make strategic decisions, but who can decide on a course of action that needs to be taken in the future. Examples of these managers include those at the Single Person, Computer System, Team Decision, Structure Group Decision, Structure Organizational and Meta-Organizational Decision Structure, Unilateral Negotiated, Consensus-Based Multiple Decision Makers, and Individual Decision Maker levels (Brândaş, 2007).

Operational decisions: These types of decisions have an impact on the organization's current activities only; they have no bearing on future activities. Only those activities, resources, or goals that have already been decided by strategic and tactical decisions are subject to operational decisions. Typically, these decisions are made by employees who are not managers of the company or by lower levels of management.

The figure below shows the level of decision (Figure 1.2).

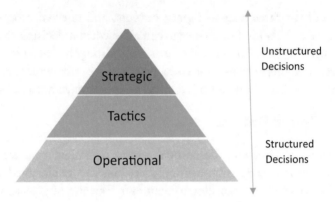

Figure 1.2: The structure and level of decision-making.

1.2.3. The Number of Decision Makers

An additional method of categorizing decision-making techniques is based on the quantity of decision-makers engaged in the process. Making decisions affects every aspect of human life, from individual decisions to corporate strategies. One can approach the decision-making process individually or cooperatively in groups. Decision-making can be categorized into two groups according to the number of decision makers:

- Individual decision-making process.
- Group decision-making.

Both individual and group decision-making impact the quality and effectiveness of the decisions made.

Individual Decision-Making: The process by which an individual evaluates a problem, weighs the options, and decides on the best course of action without consulting anybody else is known as individual decision-making. This method is frequently used for making personal decisions, such as selecting a profession, making purchases, or deciding how to handle moral dilemmas.

Group Decision Making: During the decision-making process, group decision making (GDM) is a vital component of the process and plays a critical role in human life. It can be viewed as a situation where DMs must choose the best option from a range of options while taking their preferences and viewpoints into consideration. The entire group is now accountable for the final solution rather than just one DM (Ming & Huchang, 2021). The selection procedure, in which the best option is chosen without taking into account the consensus among DMs, is the traditional focus of the GDM. Finding a collective solution that is approved by all or the majority of the DMs is crucial in practical GDM challenges (Singh, Baranwal, & Tripathi, 2023).

1.3. Types of Decision-Making Models

There are various types of decision-making models, as discussed below (Nickel, 2022):

- Rational Decision-making Model.
- Intuitive Decision-making Model.
- Creative Decision-making Model.
- Recognition-Primed Decision-making Model.

1.3.1. Rational Decision-Making Model

The classic Decision-making model is the rational Decision-making model. This model enables decision-makers to anticipate issues that are most important to them and make the best decisions for their standards.

In the rational decision-making model, decision-makers may not always know what they want or lack the necessary knowledge about the existing alternatives. Therefore, in this kind of model, decisions that decision-makers make are usually "good enough" rational decision-making consists of 8 steps is shown in Figure 1.3.

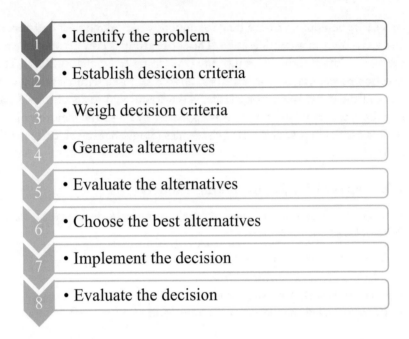

Figure 1.3: Rational decision-making model.

1.3.2. Intuitive Decision-Making Model

Intuitive Decision-making models depend on intuition, which means years of experience, expertise, educational level, and information that others cannot know. Intuition also helps with the integration of isolated data, facts, or shapes into the decision problem. Another distinctive feature of this model is that decision makers are involved in the problem detection and analysis process. The role of institutions in intuitive decision-making model is shown in Figure 1.4.

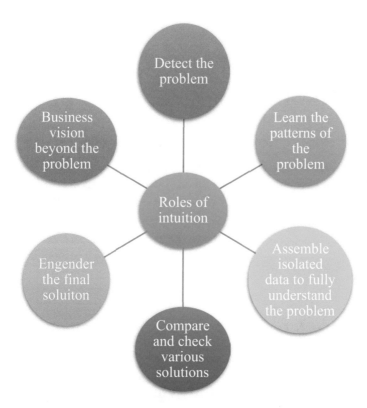

Figure 1.4: Roles of intuition in intuitive decision-making mode.

1.3.3. Creative Decision-Making Model

The creative decision-making approach is utilized when the decision maker is required to generate an innovative and distinct decision for a given situation. Having gathered the necessary information and insights about a problem and thought about some initial ideas, the decision maker goes through an incubation process where he lets his mind wander rather than think about the problem. In the end, the solution will naturally be generated, and then the testing and finalization of the answer will follow. An inherent limitation of this paradigm is that its effectiveness is mostly contingent upon the personal attributes of the decision maker, such as their level of inventiveness, as well as the specific contextual circumstances. The creative decision-making model is shown in Figure 1.5.

Figure 1.5: Creative decision-making model.

1.3.4. Recognition-Primed Decision-Making Model

Recognition-primed decision model incorporates contextual assessment and mental evaluation to come up with the best reaction to a problem. In this model, decision makers evaluate one alternative rather than evaluating more than one at the same time. The success rate of the recognition-primed decision-making model is related to the expertise and experience of a manager and is preferred in cases of time limitations. The recognition-primed decision-making model can be seen in Figure 1.6.

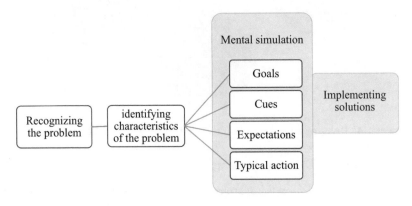

Figure 1.6: Recognition-primed decision-making model.

1.4. Types of Decision-Making Problem

Decision-making can be divided into two types based on the type of decision problem: single criterion and multi-criteria decision-making (MCDM) (Figure 1.7) (Triantaphyllou, 2000).

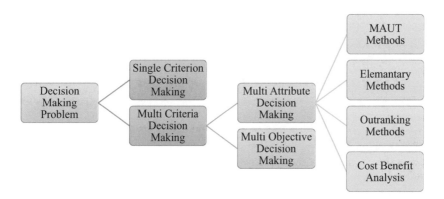

Figure 1.7: Type of decision-making problem.

Single criterion decision-making is the process of selecting the best alternative from a set of alternatives based on a single criterion. For example, if you are choosing between two new cars, you might use the criterion of price to make your decision.

MCDM is the process of selecting the best alternative from a set of alternatives based on multiple criteria. For example, if you are choosing between two new jobs, you might consider criteria such as salary, benefits, work-life balance, and location. The key differences between single criterion and multi-criteria decision-making are shown in Table 1.1 below.

Table 1.1: The Key Differences Between Single Criterion and Multi-Criteria Decision-Making

Characteristic	Single criterion decision-making	Multi-criteria decision-making (MCDM)
Number of criteria	One	Two or more
Complexity	Simpler	More complex
Realism	Less realistic	More realistic
Common applications	Simple decision problems, such as choosing the cheapest product or the fastest route	Complex decision problems, such as choosing a new job or investment opportunity

1.4.1. Decision Problem and Its Characteristics

A decision problem is a situation in which a decision-maker must choose one alternative from a set of alternatives.

Decision problems can be characterized by a number of factors, including:

Decision maker:	This is the person or group who makes the decision among existing alternatives.
Aim (to be achieved):	They are the outcomes of the decision maker's actions.
Criterion:	It is the value system that the decision maker uses to select an option.
Alternatives and strategies:	These are the different actions that can be chosen by the decision maker. They depend on the resources that are under the control of the decision maker and are controllable.
Events:	The events that are possible to happen in the future are called "nature state". These variables are all environmental variables, and they are not under the decision maker's control.
Outcome:	It reflects the value obtained from each alternative and event. The outcomes are presented in the form of tables (matrix) or tree diagrams.

Representation of decision problems:

(a) **Decision matrix (Solution Matrix or Decision Model):** Decision matrix is a set of data represented in rows and columns as a grid. The values measured by the decision matrix is called "dependent variable $\left(O_{ij}\right)$". Controllable variables are strategies (alternatives) $\left(S_i\right)$ while uncontrollable ones are events $\left(N_j\right)$. Both controllable and uncontrollable parameters constitute the "independent variables".

(b) The dimensions of the decision matrix can be found through determining the outcome by O_{ij} while "i" representing the alternatives and "j" representing the events. Therefore, the dependent variable O_{ij} is the function of independent variables S_i and $N_j : O_{ij} = f\left(S_i, N_j\right)$. The decision matrix is shown in Table 1.2 below.

Table 1.2: The Decision Matrix

	Probability/Event			
	P_1	P_2	....	P_m
	N_1	N_2	......	N_m
S_1	O_{11}	O_{12}	......	O_{1m}
S_2	O_{21}	O_{22}	......	O_{2m}
S_3	O_{31}	O_{32}	......	O_{3m}
.	...	...	......	...
S_n	O_{n1}	O_{n2}	......	O_{nm}

Strategies

(c) **Decision tree:** Another method of representing decision problems is the decision tree, which is constructed via a technique called "tree diagram" Compared to the decision matrix, the decision tree enables the problem to be represent much simpler and clearer. It is a graphic map of all the elements in a matrix, which is shown in Figure 1.8.

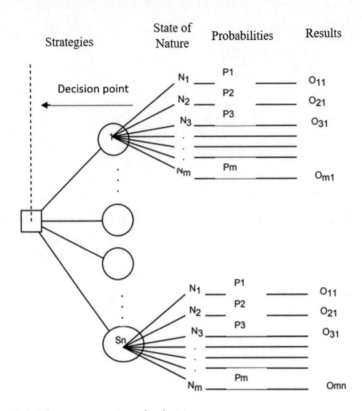

Figure 1.8: The representation of a decision tree.

As shown in Figure 1.8, decision models which have one decision point are called "single-stage decision models". These models can be represented as decision matrixes or trees. However, if there are more decision points in a process, then "multi-stage decision models" are used. Since multi-stage decision models consist of many decision points, they should be represented as decision trees. A decision tree regarding the two-stage decision problem is shown in Figure 1.9 below.

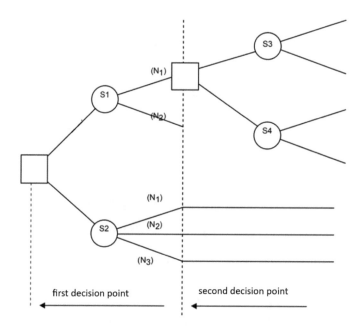

Figure 1.9: A two-stage decision tree.

1.5. Multi-Criteria Decision-Making

As it was mentioned previously, decision problems involving more than one criterion are called "Multi-Criteria Decision-Making (MCDM)." There are various methods to solve MCDM problems. The common feature of these methods is that they provide the maximum benefit to the decision maker by enabling them to choose the most suitable alternative among many. MCDM methods are also used for different purposes, among which sorting and classifying are the most common.

In order to choose the best decision-making method for a problem, it is of utmost importance to understand the decision-making classification (Sabaei, Erkoyuncu, & Roy, 2015). For general categorization of MCDM methods, in the first step MCDM can be categorized as Figure 1.10 (Hwang & Masud, 1979).

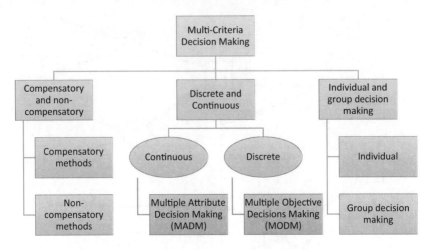

Figure 1.10: MCDM category based on data processing.

In the realm of MCDM techniques, there are two primary categories: Multiple Objective Decision-making (MODM) and Multiple Attribute Decision-making (MADM) (Sabaei, Erkoyuncu, & Roy, 2015; Hassan, Tan, & Yusof, 2016)

• Multi attribute decision-making (MADM)
  MADM techniques are designed for the selection of alternatives from a pool of feasible options, each characterized by multiple attributes.
• Multi objective decision-making (MODM)
  MODM techniques build upon the foundation of linear programming. It involved linear expressions in single objective function and constraints, in which continuous decision variables are used. However, MODM techniques introduce the concept of multi-objective functions, where multiple objectives are considered simultaneously within the model.

A comparison between MODM and MADM has been presented in Table 1.3.

Table 1.3: Comparison of MODM and MADM

Feature	MADM	MODM
Criteria defined by	Attribute/Criterion	Objective
Model basis	Alternative identification and specification	Target objectives and interrelationship between evaluating criteria
Objectives	Implicit	Explicit
Alternatives	Finite number	Infinite number
Attributes	Finite field	Infinite field
Decision space	Discrete	Continuous
Decision maker's control	Limited	Significant
Decision-making paradigm	Outcome oriented	Process oriented
Relevant application	Selection/Evaluation	Design/Research

When it comes to maintenance management, there are a limited number of feasible solutions, and the category that must be selected is MADM (Multi-Attribute Decision Making). It is crucial to take an additional step in categorizing approaches in order to select the most suitable method based on the type of problem.

MADM is classified according to the type of data processing in order to determine the most appropriate approach based on the behavior of the attributes. Figure 1.11 depicts this category. (Sabaei, Erkoyuncu, & Roy, 2015).

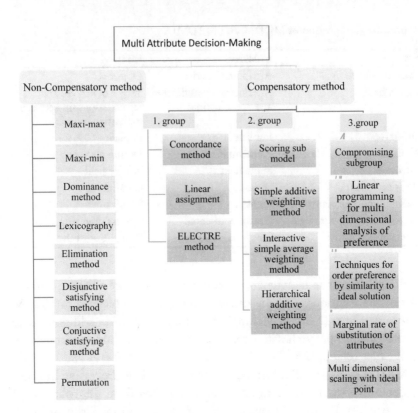

Figure 1.11: MADM category based on data processing.

Due to the various perspectives from which maintenance management criteria can be developed, it is not possible to select acceptable approaches solely based on the data processing point of view. Data availability can also be a determining factor in choosing the most appropriate strategy. The categorization has been depicted in Figure 1.12 (Sabaei, Erkoyuncu, & Roy, 2015).

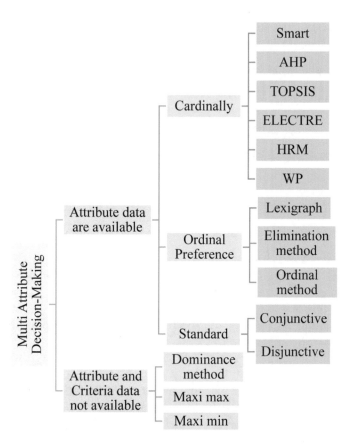

Figure 1.12: MADM methods categorized in data availability perspective.

Effective and helpful decisions, in situations when several factors are present, were considered standard practice from the start of the 1960s and were reinforced by daily work. For this reason, numerous techniques have been created. They differ from each other in terms of the required quality and quantity of supplementary information necessary, the user-friendliness of the procedures and the software they are associated with, and the mathematical qualities (Turskis & Zavadskas, 2011). None of these methods are superior to others, nor are they capable of responding to the whole range of MCDM problems. For this reason, hybrid approaches are generally preferred for complex problems involving various types of uncertainty.

MCDM can also be categorized by a number of answers (Hwang & Masud, 1979), (Li & Wang, 2007);

- Innumerable when the admissible answers are infinite and
- Numerable when admissible answers are finite.

1.5.1. Analyzing MCDM Methods

MCDM Methods are based on Decision Theory in which decisions are made to reach the final objective under a set of decision-making alternatives.

1.5.1.1. Strengths of MCDM Methods

The strengths are enlisted as below (Chatterjee, 2013):

(a) It is open and clear.
(b) Objectives and criteria for decision-making can be reviewed and changed if felt to be incorrect.
(c) Multiple objectives can be addressed simultaneously.
(d) The multi-disciplinary approach can be used to various real-life decision-making scenarios.
(e) It has a systemic approach, demonstrating compromises between the adverse issues.
(f) It provides a method of communication both within the decision-making group and with the wider community.
(g) The ratings and weights are explicit and created using well-established methodologies. These can also be cross-referenced with other sources of relative value information and updated as needed.
(h) It is a practical decision-making process that enables real life subjectivity and experience of the decision makers.
(i) It enables people to understand what the consequences of assigning a different order of importance to different objectives or making different assessments to the performance of the available options against different objectives would be.
(j) It facilitates appraisal-led design, where the appraisal is refined during the design process.
(k) It facilitates structuring a management problem properly.
(l) The model serves as a basis for discussion.
(m) It offers a process that leads to rational, justifiable, and explainable decisions.

(n) It speeds up problem solving procedures in any organization.

(o) It can deal with mixed data, including quantitative and qualitative measurements.

(p) It promotes a participatory planning and decision-making system.

(q) The decision-making process is transparent and productive, allowing for a greater understanding of the problem and more effective negotiation.

(r) It eliminates personal bias in selecting an alternative.

(s) It enhances understanding of goals and issues.

(t) It accurately assesses the chosen decision criteria.

(u) It encourages consensus-building on the optimal solution.

(v) It assesses decision-making preferences for each criterion, balancing conflicting criteria and ensuring cost-effectiveness.

(w) It promotes consensus and compromise among decision-making alternatives, favoring competing options.

An illustration of a MCDM process is given Figure 1.13 (Belton & Theodor, 2002).

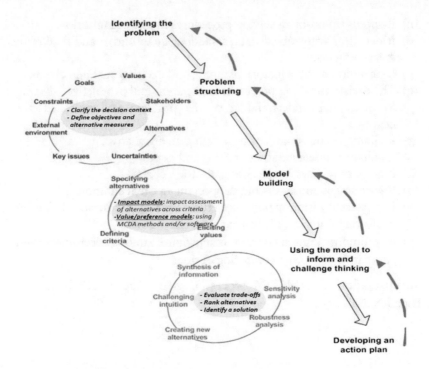

Figure 1.13: An illustration of a MCDM process.

1.5.1.2. *Weaknesses of MCDM Methods*

The weaknesses of MCDM Methods will be explained in detail in Chapter 3.

Chapter 2   Commonly Applied MCDM Methods

In this chapter, some of the most published MCDM METHods, such as ELECTRE, TOPSIS, VIKOR, and PROMETHEE, will be thoroughly examined (Basílio, Pereira, Costa, Santos, & Ghosh, 2022) (Krstic, Agnusdei, Miglietta, Tadic, & Roso, 2022).

2.1. ELECTRE

The ELECTRE (ELimination Et Choix Traduisant la REalite´-ELimination and Choice Expressing the REality) method was introduced by Benayoun, Roy et al. in 1966. It aimed to select the best option among a set of alternatives, and then later, it was named ELECTRE I. There followed many variations of this method in the following years, such as ELECTRE II (Roy & Bertier, 1973), ELECTRE III (Roy B. , 1978), ELECTRE IV (Roy & Hugonnard, 1982), ELECTRE TRI (Yu, 1992) and ELECTRE IS (Roy & Skalka, 1984), which served as a solution to problems such as choosing, ranking or ordering. In this study, ELECTRE III will be discussed. ELECTRE III method, consists of the following steps:

2.1.1. Steps of ELECTRE III

Step 1: Creating the decision matrix: To record data, a decision matrix D can be created and expressed as follows (Equation 2.1). Where each A_i represent alternative i $(i = 1, 2, …, m)$ considered; C_j $(j = 1, 2, …, n)$ is the criterion used to measure the performance of each alternative; and x_{ij} is the rating of the i-th alternative with respect to the j-th criterion.

$$
D = \begin{array}{c} \\ A_1 \\ \vdots \\ A_i \\ \vdots \\ A_m \end{array} \overset{\displaystyle C_1 \; \cdots \; C_j \; \cdots \; C_n}{\begin{bmatrix} x_{11} \cdots & x_{12} \cdots & x_{1n} \\ & & \vdots \\ x_{i1} \cdots & x_{ij} \cdots & x_{in} \\ & & \vdots \\ x_{m1} \cdots & x_{mj} \cdots & x_{mn} \end{bmatrix}} \qquad (2.1)
$$

Step 2: Establishment of the standard decision matrix: The Standard Decision Matrix is a matrix created by using the elements of matrix D and using the following formula (Equation 2.2).

$$r_{ij} = \frac{x_{ij}}{\sqrt{\sum_{k=1}^{m} x_{kj}^2}} \tag{2.2}$$

The R matrix to be obtained with the help of the formula is obtained as follows in (Equation 2.3):

$$R_{ij} = \begin{bmatrix} r_{11} & r_{12} & \cdots & r_{1n} \\ r_{21} & r_{22} & \cdots & r_{2n} \\ \cdot & \cdot & \cdot & \cdot \\ \cdot & \cdot & \cdot & \cdot \\ \cdot & \cdot & \cdot & \cdot \\ r_{m1} & r_{m2} & \cdots & r_{mn} \end{bmatrix} \tag{2.3}$$

Step 3: Establishing the weighted standard decision matrix: The significance of assessment elements may vary depending on the decision maker. The V matrix is computed to accurately represent the notable disparities in the ELECTRE solution. Prior to making a decision, the individual in charge must initially ascertain the weights (w_j) assigned to the assessment elements. The variable wj represents the subjective assessment of the significance of the j-th criterion, as determined by the decision makers. Next, the elements in each column of the matrix R are multiplied by the corresponding values of w_j to create the matrix V. The matrix V is displayed in Equation (2.4) below:

$$V_{ij} = \begin{bmatrix} w_1 r_{11} & w_2 r_{12} & \cdots & w_n r_{1n} \\ w_1 r_{21} & w_2 r_{22} & \cdots & w_n r_{2n} \\ \cdot & \cdot & \cdot & \cdot \\ \cdot & \cdot & \cdot & \cdot \\ \cdot & \cdot & \cdot & \cdot \\ w_1 r_{m1} & w_2 r_{m2} & \cdots & w_n r_{mn} \end{bmatrix} \tag{2.4}$$

Step 4: Determination of concordance and discordance sets: After that, concordance and discordance sets are determined. For each pair of alternatives A_p and $Aq\,(p,\ q = 1, 2, \ldots,\ m\ and,\ p \neq q)$, the set of criteria is divided into two distinct subsets. In terms of the criteria against which alternative A_p is preferred to alternative A_q the concordance set is composed as in (Equation 2.5):

$$C_{pq} = \left\{ j, v_{pj} \geq v_{qj} \right\} \qquad (2.5)$$

C_{pq} represents the set of attributes where A_p is superior to or at least equal to A_q. After finishing the calculation of C_{pq}, the discordance set D_{pq} can be derived by examining the criteria that determine when A_p is superior to A_q. It can be expressed as shown in Equation (2.6).

$$D_{pq} = \left\{ j, v_{pj} \geq v_{qj} \right\} \qquad (2.6)$$

The number of concordances sets in the MCDM problem is $\left(m^2 - m\right)$. Because p and q indices must be $p \neq q$ when constructing concordance sets. The number of elements in a concordance set can be up to the number of evaluation factors (n). When creating concordance sets, the positive or negative effects of the criteria must be considered.

Step 5: Establishment of concordance and discordance matrices: Concordance sets are used to generate the concordance matrix (C). The C matrix is dimensioned $m \times n$ and does not take values for $p = q$. The matrix C is shown in (2.7) below:

$$C = \begin{bmatrix} - & c_{12} & c_{13} & \cdots & c_{1m} \\ c_{21} & - & c_{23} & \cdots & c_{2m} \\ \cdot & \cdot & \cdot & \cdot & \cdot \\ \cdot & \cdot & \cdot & \cdot & \cdot \\ \cdot & \cdot & \cdot & \cdot & \cdot \\ c_{m1} & c_{m2} & c_{m3} & \cdots & - \end{bmatrix} \qquad (2.7)$$

The elements of the matrix C are calculated using the relation shown in the following form (Equation 2.8).

$$c_{pq} = \sum_{j \in C_{pq}} w_j \tag{2.8}$$

The elements of the discordance matrix (D) are calculated using the following formula:

$$d_{pq} = \frac{\max\limits_{j \in D_{pq}} \left| v_{pj} - v_{qj} \right|}{\max\limits_{j} \left| v_{pj} - v_{qj} \right|} \tag{2.9}$$

The discordance index d_{pq} quantifies the level of disagreement in $A_p \rightarrow A_q$, where A_p outranks A_q, indicating that the performance values of A_p are either better or at least equivalent to those of A_q across the majority of criteria. Similar to matrix C, matrix D is also of size $m x m$ and does not have any values for $p = q$. The matrix D is represented as given in Equation (2.10) below:

$$D = \begin{bmatrix} - & d_{12} & d_{13} & \cdots & d_{1m} \\ d_{21} & - & d_{23} & \cdots & d_{2m} \\ . & . & . & . & . \\ . & . & . & . & . \\ . & . & . & . & . \\ d_{m1} & d_{m2} & d_{m3} & \cdots & - \end{bmatrix} \tag{2.10}$$

Step 6: Establishment of concordance superiority and disconcordance superiority matrices: The $m \times m$ dimensional concordance **superiority** matrix (F) is obtained as a result of comparing the **concordance** threshold value $\underline{c}$ with the elements of the concordance matrix (c_{pq}). The **concordance** threshold value $\underline{c}$, also defined as the average compliance index, is calculated using the following formula in (2.11):

$$\underline{c} = \frac{1}{m(m-1)} \sum_{p=1}^{m} \sum_{q=1}^{m} c_{pq} \tag{2.11}$$

F matrix is a matrice consisting of 1 or 0 values of elements (f_q for $p \neq q$) other than diagonal values $(p \neq q)$, as in C and D matrices. It is decided according to the conditions of

"IF $c_{pq} \geq \underline{c} \Rightarrow f_{pq} = 1$ " and "IF $c_{pq} < \underline{c} \Rightarrow f_{pq} = 0$" that one of these elements will have a value of 1 and others will have a value of 0.

The **disconcordance** superiority matrix (G) is also an *mxn* dimensional matrix and is generated in a manner like F matrix. The **disconcordance** threshold value $(\underline{d})$ is obtained by the following formula in (Equation 2.12):

$$d = \frac{1}{m(m-1)} \sum_{p=1}^{n} \sum_{q=1}^{n} d_{pq} \qquad (2.12)$$

The diagonal elements (g_{pq}) of the matrix G also take the value 1 or 0. Which element takes the value will be determined according to the " IF $d_{pq} \geq \underline{d} \Rightarrow g_{pq} = 1$ " and " IF $d_{pq} < \underline{d} \Rightarrow g_{pq} = 0$ " conditions.

Step 7: Formation of the total dominance matrix: The elements (e_{pq}) of the total dominance matrix (E) are equal to the reciprocal multiplication of the elements f_{pq} and g_{pq}, as shown in the following form (Equation 2.13). E matrix, like C and D matrices, is an $m \times n$ dimensional matrix that does not have diagonal elements and whose elements outside the diagonal are 1 or 0.

$$e_{pq} = f_{pq} \cdot g_{pq} \qquad (2.13)$$

Step 8: Determination of importance of decision: The rows and columns of matrix E show the decision points. For example, if E matrix is calculated as follows in (Equation 2.14), then the elements of the E matrix are $e_{21} = 1$ and $e_{32} = 1$.

$$E = \begin{bmatrix} - & 0 & 0 \\ 1 & - & 0 \\ 1 & 1 & - \end{bmatrix} \qquad (2.14)$$

This shows the absolute superiority of the second decision point to the first decision point, the third decision point to the first decision point, and the third decision point to the second decision point. In this case, if the decision points are represented by a symbol A_i $(i = 1,2,...m)$ the order of importance of the decision points will be A_3 , A_2 and A_1 .

2.2. PROMETHEE

Brans developed the PROMETHEE (Preference Ranking Organization METHods for Enrichment Evaluation) approach in 1982, which includes PROMETHEE I for partial ranking of alternatives, PROMETHEE II for complete ranking, PROMETHEE III for interval ranking, and PROMETHEE IV for continuous viable solutions (Brans, 1982). Other members include PROMETHEE V (Brans & Mareschal, 1992), PROMETHEE VI (Brans & Mareschal, 1995), PROMETHEE GDSS (Macharis, Brans, & Mareschal., 1998), and visual interactive module GAIA (Geometrical Analysis for Interactive Aid) for graphical representation (Brans & Mareschal, 2005), etc.

PROMETHEE II, which presents the fundamental to the implementation of other PROMETHEE methods, consists of the following steps (Behzadian, Kazemzadeh, Albadvi, & Aghdasi, 2010):

2.2.1. Steps of PROMETHEE II

Step 1: Determination of deviations based on pairwise comparisons.

$$d_j(a,b) = g_j(a) - g_j(b) \qquad (2.15)$$

where, a and b are two alternatives, and $d_j(a,b)$ denotes the difference between the evaluations of a and b on each criterion (assuming there are m alternatives and n criteria) (Equation 2.15).

Step 2: Application of the preference function

$$P_j(a,b) = F_j\left[d_j(a,b)\right], \quad j = 1,2,...,n \qquad (2.16)$$

The notation $P_j(a,b)$ represents the reference of option an in relation to alternative b with respect to the j-th criterion. This reference is determined by the function $d_j(a,b)$ as defined in Equation (2.16). The implementation of the method includes six distinct preference functions: the first type (ordinary), the second type (U-type), the third type (V-type), the fourth type (level), the fifth type (linear), and the sixth type (Gaussian).

Step 3: Calculation of an overall or global preference index

$$\pi(a,b) = \sum_{j=1}^{n} P_j(a,b)w_j, \quad \forall a,b \in A \qquad (2.17)$$

where, $\pi(a,b)$ of a over b (from 0 to 1) is defined as the weighted sum of $p(a, b)$ for each criterion, and w_j is the weight of the j-th criterion (Equation 2.17).

Step 4: Calculation of the positive and negative outranking flows (the PROMETHEE I partial ranking)

$$\varphi^+(a) = \frac{1}{m-1}\sum_{x \in A}\pi(a,x) \qquad (2.18)$$

$$\varphi^-(a) = \frac{1}{m-1}\sum_{x \in A}\pi(x,a) \qquad (2.19)$$

In Equation (2.18), $\varphi^+(a)$ represents the positive outranking flow for each alternative, while in Equation (2.19), $\varphi^-(a)$ represents the negative outranking flow for each alternative. The partial outranking can be derived from the two rankings generated by $\varphi^+(a)$ and $\varphi^-(a)$. a outranks b if and only if the positive φ-value of an is greater than or equal to the positive φ-value of b, and the negative φ-value of b is less than or equal to the negative φ-value of a. Alternatively, the outcome may lead to an indifference connection or an inability to compare the two possibilities.

Step 5: Calculation of net outranking flow (the PROMETHEE II complete ranking)

$$\varphi(a) = \varphi^+(a) - \varphi^-(a) \qquad (2.20)$$

where $\varphi(a)$ denotes the net outranking flow for each alternative in (2.20). The higher the net flow is, the better the alternative.

2.3. TOPSIS

Hwang and Yoon developed the TOPSIS (Technique for Order Preference by Similarity to an Ideal Solution) method in (1981). The technique relies on the concept that the selected option should have the highest Euclidean distance from the negative ideal solution (NIS) and the lowest distance from the positive ideal solution (PIS).

2.3.1. Steps of TOPSIS

The steps of the method are given below (Taşabat, 2019).

Step 1. Determining the decision matrix as in (Equation 2.21):

$$X = \begin{bmatrix} x_{11} & x_{12} & \cdots & x_{1m} \\ x_{21} & x_{22} & \cdots & x_{2m} \\ & & \vdots & \\ \cdots & \cdots & x_{ij} & \cdots \\ x_{n1} & x_{n2} & \cdots & x_{nm} \end{bmatrix} \qquad (2.21)$$

A general multiple criteria analysis problem is represented as a decision matrix which consists of a set of alternatives $A_i \ (i = 1, 2, ..., n)$ to be evaluated against a set of criteria $C_j \ (j = 1, 2, ..., m)$.

Step 2. Determining the weighting vector as in (Equation 2.22) below:

$$W = \left(w_1, \cdots, w_j, \cdots, w_m \right) \qquad (2.22)$$

In which w_j represents the relative importance of criterion C_j in relation to the problem's overall objective.

Step 3. Normalizing the decision matrix through Euclidean normalization (Equation 2.23):

$$x'_{ij} = \frac{x_{ij}}{\left(\sum_{k=1}^{n} x_{ik}^2 \right)^{1/2}} \qquad (2.23)$$

As a result, a normalized decision matrix can be determined as in (Equation 2.24):

$$X' = \begin{bmatrix} x_{11}{}' & x_{12}{}' & \cdots & x_{1m}{}' \\ x_{21}{}' & x_{22}{}' & \cdots & x_{2m}{}'^2 \\ & & \vdots & \\ \cdots & \cdots & x_{ij}{}' & \cdots \\ x_{n1}{}' & x_{n2}{}' & \cdots & x_{nm}{}' \end{bmatrix}$$

(2.24)

Step 4. Calculating the performance matrix as in (Equation 2.25):

$$Y = \begin{bmatrix} w_1 x_{11}{}' & w_2 x_{12}{}' & \cdots & w_m x_{1m}{}' \\ w_1 x_{21}{}' & w_2 x_{22}{}' & \cdots & w_m x_{2m}{}'^2 \\ & & \vdots & \\ \cdots & \cdots & w_i x_{ij}{}' & \cdots \\ w_1 x_{n1}{}' & w_2 x_{n2}{}' & \cdots & w_m x_{nm}{}' \end{bmatrix} = \begin{bmatrix} y_{11} & y_{12} & \cdots & y_{1m} \\ y_{21} & y_{22} & \cdots & y_{2m} \\ & & \vdots & \\ \cdots & \cdots & y_{ij} & \cdots \\ y_{n1} & y_{n2} & \cdots & y_{nm} \end{bmatrix}$$

(2.25)

The weighted performance matrix is obtained by multiplying the normalized decision matrix (Equation 2.24) with the weight vector (Equation 2.25). This matrix provides information about the performance of each alternative with respect to each criterion.

Step 5. Determining the PIS and the NIS:

The Positive Ideal Solution (PIS) (Equation 2.26) and Negative Ideal Solution (NIS) (Equation 2.27) are the best or worst criteria values possible among all possibilities. Deng (2007) identified several benefits of using these two notions, including their simplicity and comprehensibility, computing efficiency, and ability to quantify the relative performance of alternatives in a simple mathematical manner. Consider $PIS(I^+)$:

$$I^+ = \left\{ (max_i y_{ij} \mid j \in J), (min_i y_{ij} \mid j \in J') \right\}$$

(2.26)

$$I^+ = \left\{ y_1^+, y_2^+, \cdots, y_n^+ \right\}$$

And for $NIS(I^-)$:

$$I^- = \left\{ (min_i y_{ij} \mid j \in J), (max_i y_{ij} \mid j \in J') \right\}$$

(2.27)

$$I^- = \left\{ y_1^-, y_2^-, \cdots, y_n^- \right\}$$

J and J' show the benefit (maximization) and loss (minimization) values, respectively, at both formulas.

Step 6. Calculating the degree of distance of the alternatives between each alternative and the PIS and the NIS:

The D^+ and the D^- formulas are as the follow respectively in (Equation 2.28) and (Equation 2.29), by using Euclidean distance.

$$D_i^+ = \sqrt{\sum_{j=1}^{n}\left(y_{ij} - y_j^+\right)^2} \tag{2.28}$$

$$D_i^- = \sqrt{\sum_{j=1}^{n}\left(y_{ij} - y_j^-\right)^2} \tag{2.29}$$

Step 7. Calculating the overall performance index for each alternative across all criteria:

This index can be calculated based on the concept of the degree of similarity of alternative Ai relative to the ideal solutions (Equation 2.30).

$$P_i = \frac{D_i^-}{D_i^- + D_i^+} \tag{2.30}$$

$0 \leq P_i \leq 1$ The P_i value indicates the absolute closeness of the ideal solution. IF $P_i = 1$ then A_i is the ideal solution, IF $P_i = 0$ then A_i is the negative ideal solution.

Step 8. Ranking the alternatives in the descending order of the performance index value.

2.4. VIKOR

In Serbian, VIKOR means for VIsekriterijumska optimizaacija i KOmpromisno Resenje, and it was invented by Serafim Opricovic, who referred to it as the compromise ranking system. VIKOR is an outranking approach for ranking and selecting a finite collection of alternative actions based on criteria. It solves a discrete multi-criteria problem with non-commensurable and competing criteria (Opricovic, 1998).

2.4.1. Steps of VIKOR

The procedure of traditional VIKOR for compromise-ranking can be described as the following steps (Qu, Wan, Yang, & Lee, 2018):

Step 1: Determine the best x_j^* and the worst x_j^- values of all criterion functions, where $j = 1, 2, \cdots, n$ are given as in (Equation 2.31):

$$x_j^* = max_j x_{ij} \text{ and } x_j^- = min_j x_{ij} \tag{2.31}$$

After these values are found, the following formula given in (Equation 2.32) is used for normalization.

$$r_{ij} = \frac{\left(x_j^* - x_{ij}\right)}{(x_j^* - x_j^-)} \tag{2.32}$$

Step 2: Compute the values of S_i (Equation 2.33) and R_i (Equation 2.34) where $= 1, 2, \cdots, m$:

$$S_i = \sum_{j=1}^{n} w_j \frac{\left(x_j^* - x_{ij}\right)}{(x_j^* - x_j^-)} \tag{2.33}$$

$$R_i = max\left[w_j \frac{x_j^* - x_{ij}}{x_j^* - x_j^-}\right] \tag{2.34}$$

S_i and R_i denote the utility measure and the regret measure, respectively, for the alternative A_i . w_j is the weight of the j-th criterion.

Step 3: Compute the value Q_i as in (Equation 2.35) where, $i = 1, 2, \cdots, m$.

$$Q_i = v\left(\frac{S_i - S^*}{S^- - S^*}\right) + (1 - v)\left(\frac{R_i - R^*}{R^- - R^*}\right) \tag{2.35}$$

$$S^* = min_i S_i, S^- = max_i S_i \text{ and } R^* = min_i R_i, R^- = max_i R_i \tag{2.36}$$

where, v is the weight for the strategy of maximum group utility and $(1 - v)$ is the weight of the individual regret. v is usually set to " 0.5 " (Opricovic, 1998).

Step 4: Rank the alternatives, sorting by the S, R and Q values in a descending order. The outcomes are three ranking lists. The lower the value of Q_i the better the decision between alternatives A_i is.

Step 5: If the next two requirements are met, suggest a compromise option, the alternative (A'), which is ranked highest by the minimum value of Q:

C1. "Acceptable advantage": $Q(A'') - Q(A') \geq D$, where A'' is the alternative with second position in the ranking list by Q; $DQ = \dfrac{1}{(j-1)}$ and m is the number of alternatives.

C2. "Acceptable stability in decision-making": The alternative A' should also be the best in terms of S and/or R value (The lower the value of S/R is, the better).

If one of these conditions is not satisfied, it is not possible to directly select the best solution for the set. Nevertheless, a subset of preferable solutions can be established, which consists of (Opricovic & Tzeng, 2007):

1. Alternatives A' and A'' if only the condition C2 is not satisfied, or

2. Alternatives $A', A'', \cdots, A^{(M)}$ if the condition C1 is not satisfied, where $A^{(M)}$ is determined by the relation $Q(A^{(M)}) - Q(A') < DQ$ for maximum M.

Chapter 3   Weaknesses of MCDM Methods

In this chapter, weaknesses of MCDM methods will be discussed in detail.

3.1. Weaknesses of MCDM Methods

The majority of MCDM methods in the literature involves the steps below:

1. Reduction of the decision matrix to the same unit (conversion strategy).
2. Specification of weights.
3. Applying the measurement method.
4. Ranking/sorting/ordering of the outcomes.

It is possible to apply different techniques and methods in these four steps. Since using a different approach in at least one of the aforementioned steps will alter the results of the selected MCDM method, these steps can also be seen as the shortcomings of MCDM approaches.

Different methods that can be used in each step of aforementioned MCDM methods are discussed under the following headings:

1. Determining the method of reducing the decision matrix to the same unit (conversion strategy).
2. Determining the method of weighting.
3. Determining (differentiating) the measurement method.
4. Determining the ranking/sorting/ordering method.

By combining the various methodologies discussed in this part with the basic phases of the MCDM procedures outlined above, numerous outcomes can be achieved. Since this is not a very desirable situation in the literature, it is described as a "weakness" within the scope of the book.

In the following sub-sections, the details of these stages, defined as weaknesses, will be discussed under the chosen MCDM methods ELECTRE, TOPSIS, VIKOR and PROMETHEE. It is possible to draw a similar inference for other MCDM methods. While the first two weaknesses mentioned above are valid for all MCDM methods, the last two weaknesses may differ depending on the content and structure of the chosen MCDM methods.

The application of different methods in the operational steps of MCDM methods is also the transformation of traditional methods into modified ones.

3.1.1. Determining the Method for Reducing the Decision Matrix to the Same Unit

Two methods are well-known for adjusting data. These are "normalization" and "standardization".

3.1.1.1. Normalization

Normalization is a technique which scales all numeric variables in the range [0, 1]. Some possible formulas of normalization are given below:

$$x'_{ij} = \frac{x_{ij}}{\left(\sum_{j=1}^{n} x_{ij}^2\right)^{1/2}} \tag{3.1}$$

$$x'_{ij} = \frac{x_{ij}}{median_X} \tag{3.2}$$

$$x'_{ij} = \frac{x_{ij}}{max(x_{ij})} \tag{3.3}$$

The normalization equalization in (Equation 3.1) is called "Euclid normalization".

3.1.1.2. Standardization

Standardization is a method which transforms the variables to have zero mean and unit variance. In Equation (3.4) below it was represented:

$$x'_{ij} = \frac{x_{ij} - \mu_x}{\sigma_x} \tag{3.4}$$

Standardization can be performed in three ways (Weller & Romney, 1990):

- **column-standardization** (variable or criteria),
- **row-standardization** (observation or alternative) and
- **double standardization** (both row and column standardization).

In **column-standardization**, variables are taken separately and data for each variable are combined into a single measure, whereas in **row-standardization**, the converse is true. That is, the observations are treated one by one, and the variables are adjusted to the same value for each observation. It is also feasible that column and row standardization take place at the same time Taşabat (2019) describes this as "**double standardization**".

3.1.1.3. Selection of Appropriate Standardization Method

The researchers can examine various facets of the underlying, fundamental structure using various data transformations. The structure may be examined "wholistically" with the main effects, interaction, and error present or the main effects may be "removed" to focus on the interaction (and error) (Weller & Romney, 1990).

These approaches can be used in sorting and grouping the alternatives. Selecting the appropriate standardization method depends on the structure of the decision problem. That is:

- **Column standardization:** If observations are important,
- **Row standardization:** If it is important to bring the variables to the same unit,
- **Double standardization:** Where both observations and variables are important to be independent of the unit, preferable.

3.1.2. Determining the Weight Assignment Method

Another crucial stage in MCDM approaches is figuring out how much weight to give performance criteria. Because varying performance rankings may result from the weights assigned to the criteria. Even small changes in weight values can often change the result significantly. Determining the weights of the criteria is therefore one of the most crucial steps in the decision-making process.

In the literature, there are many techniques for weighting of the variables. In this book, we will use "Saaty method", which depends on expert opinion and is the most frequently used and "best-worst method", which is the modified version of Saaty method. In addition, we will also use the "equal weights method", which expresses that all the alternatives have the same degree of importance. By doing so, we are aiming to emphasize the

importance of weighting in ranking the alternatives in MCDM methods. In
the sub-sections to follow, the methods mentioned above will be discussed
in detail.

3.1.2.1. Saaty's Method

Saaty method, also known as the Analytic Hierarchy Process (AHP), is a
method proposed by Thomas Saaty in 1980 (Saaty, 2008). In this method,
the model is created depending on pair-wise comparisons in line with an
expert view. The steps for AHP are stated below in detail:

Step 1: Computing the vector of criteria weights.

The AHP initiates the process of determining the weights for the various
criteria by constructing a pairwise comparison matrix A. The matrix A is
a real matrix of size $m \times m$ where m is the number of assessment criteria being examined. Each element a_{jk} of the matrix A reflects the value
located in the j-th row and k-th column of A. Let v be a vector, where v_i
represents the i-th element of v. This vector measures the significance of
the j-th criterion compared to the k-th criterion. If the value of a_{jk} is more
than 1, it indicates that the j-th criterion holds more significance than the
k-th criterion. Conversely, if the value of a_{jk} is less than 1, it implies that
the j-th criterion is of lesser importance compared to the k-th criterion. If
two criteria are equally important, then the value of the entry a_{jk} is 1. The
entries a_{jk} and a_{kj} must adhere to the following constraint:

$$a_{jk} . a_{kj} = 1 \qquad\qquad (3.5)$$

Obviously, $a_{ij} = 1$ for all j.

In order to make comparisons, it is necessary to have a numerical
scale that indicates the degree to which one element is more essential or
dominant than another in relation to the criterion or characteristic being
compared. The relative significance of two criteria is measured using a
numerical scale ranging from "1 to 9", as shown in Table 3.1. It is assumed
that the j-th criterion is either equally or more crucial than the k-th criterion (Saaty, 2008).

Table 3.1: The Fundamental Scale of Absolute Numbers

Intensity of Importance	Definition	Explanation
1	Equal importance	Two activities contribute equally to the objective
2	Weak or slight	
3	Moderate importance	Experience and judgment slightly favor one activity over another
4	Moderate plus	
5	Strong importance	Experience and judgment strongly favor one activity over another
6	Strong plus	
7	Very strong or demonstrated importance	An activity is favored very strongly over another; its dominance demonstrated in practice
8	Very, very strong	
9	Extreme importance	The evidence favoring one activity over another is of the highest possible order of affirmation
Reciprocals of above	If activity I has one of the above non-zero numbers assigned to it when compared with activity j, then j has the reciprocal value when compared with I	A reasonable assumption
1.1–1.9	If the activities are very close	May be difficult to assign the best value but when compared with other contrasting activities the size of the small numbers would not be too noticeable, yet they can still indicate the relative importance of the activities.

After constructing matrix, A, it is feasible to obtain the normalized pairwise comparison matrix A_{norm} by ensuring that the total of entries in each column is equal to 1. In other words, each element $\bar{a}_{jk}$ of matrix A_{norm} is calculated as follows:

$$\overline{a}_{jk} = \frac{a_{jk}}{\sum_{l=1}^{m} a_{lk}} \tag{3.6}$$

The criteria weight vector w, which is an m-dimensional column vector, is constructed by taking the average of the elements on each row of A_{norm}.

$$w_j = \frac{\sum_{l}^{m} \overline{a}_{jl}}{m} \tag{3.7}$$

Step 2: Computing the matrix of option scores.

The matrix of option scores is a real matrix S with dimensions $n \times m$. Each element s_{ij} in S denotes the score of the i-th choice in relation to the j-th criterion. To calculate these scores, a matrix for pairwise comparisons is constructed for each of the m criteria, $j = 1, 2, \cdots, m$. The matrix $B^{(j)}$ is an $n \times n$ matrix composed of real numbers, where n represents the total number of possibilities that have been assessed. Each element $b_{ih}^{(j)}$ of the matrix indicates the assessment of the i-th choice relative to the h-th choice in terms of the j-th criterion. If the value of $b_{ih}^{(j)}$ is more than 1, it indicates that the i-th alternative is superior to the h-th option. Conversely, if $b_{ih}^{(j)}$ is less than 1, it implies that the i-th option is inferior to the h-th option. If two alternatives are determined to be equal in terms of the j-th criterion, then the value of $b_{ih}^{(j)}$ is 1. The entries $b_{ih}^{(j)}$ and $b_{hi}^{(j)}$ must adhere to the following constraint:

$$b_{ih}^{(j)} b_{hi}^{(j)} = 1 \tag{3.8}$$

All values of $b_{ii}^{(j)}$ are equal to 1 for every i. A rating system akin to the one presented in Table 3.1 can be employed to convert the decision maker's comparative assessments into numerical values.

The AHP uses the identical two-step approach to each matrix $B^{(j)}$ as stated for the pairwise comparison matrix A. This involves dividing each entry by the total of the entries in the same column, and then averaging the elements on each row. The result is the score vectors $s^{(j)}$, where $j = 1, 2, \cdots, m$. The vector $s^{(j)}$ represents the scores assigned to the evaluated choices based on the j-th criterion.

Finally, the score matrix S is obtained as

$$S = \left[s^{(1)} \cdots s^{(m)} \right] \qquad (3.9)$$

i.e., the j-th column of S corresponds to $s^{(j)}$.

Step 3: Ranking the options.

Once the weight vector w and the score matrix S have been computed, the AHP obtains a vector v of global scores by multiplying S and w, i.e.

$$v = S.w \qquad (3.10)$$

The i-th entry v_i of v represents the global score assigned by the AHP to the i-th option. The option ranking is completed by arranging the global scores in descending order as the last step.

Step 4: Checking the consistency.

The Consistency Index (CI) is calculated by first determining the scalar x, which is the average of the elements in a vector. Each element in the vector is the ratio of the corresponding element in vector A_w to the corresponding element in vector w. Then,

$$CI = \frac{x - m}{m - 1} \qquad (3.11)$$

A perfectly consistent decision maker should always obtain $CI = 0$, but small values of inconsistency may be tolerated. In particular, if

$$\frac{CI}{RI} < 0.1 \qquad (3.12)$$

The inconsistencies are tolerable, and a reliable result may be expected from the AHP. In (Equation 3.12) RI is the Random Index, i.e., the consistency index when the entries of A are completely random. The values of RI for small problems (m ≤ 10) are shown in Table 3.2 (Yücel & Taşabat, 2019).

Table 3.2: Values of the RI for Small Problems

m	2	3	4	5	6	7	8	9	10
RI	0.00	0.58	0.90	1.12	1.24	1.32	1.41	1.45	1.51

Only the computation of the confidence interval CI value for matrix A is provided here. Matrix $B^{(j)}$ can also be evaluated using the same method, but with A replaced by $B^{(j)}$, w replaced by $S^{(j)}$, and m replaced by

3.1.2.2. Best-Worst Method

Different methods have been developed for solving MCDM problems. One of these methods is the best-worst method introduced by Rezaei in 2015. The method is a modified version of the AHP method, and comparisons are made only on the best and worst alternatives. The steps of the method are given below (Rezaei, 2015, 2016):

Evaluating the performance of district managers has a substantial influence on the outcome of the business's bottom line. Like other approaches, it possesses both benefits and drawbacks. The BWM offers quicker comparison times and yields more consistent and reliable results compared to the AHP (Xiaomei, Ming, Huchang, Wenjing, & Lev, 2019). Furthermore, the BWM exclusively uses integer integers for pairwise comparisons. However, similar to other subjective approaches, its effectiveness relies on the subjective evaluations made by DMs, which might be biased and lead to inaccurate outcomes. The steps for BWM are stated below in detail:

Step 1. Determine a set of decision criteria.

$$\left\{ c_1, c_2, ..., c_n \right\} \tag{3.13}$$

Step 2. Determine the best (e.g., most desirable, most important) and the worst (e.g., least desirable, least important) criteria. If more than one criterion is thought to be the best or **the worst, one can be picked arbitrarily.**

Step 3. Use a number between *"1 and 9"* to indicate your preference for the best criterion over all others. The resulting Best-to-Others vector could be:

$$A_B = \left(a_{B1}, \ a_{B2}, ..., a_{Bn} \right) \tag{3.14}$$

where a_{Bj} indicates the preference of the best criterion B over criterion J. It is clear that $a_{BB} = 1$.

Step 4. Determine the preference of all the criteria over the worst criterion using a number between 1 and 9. The resulting Others-to-Worst vector would be:

$$A_W = (a_{1W}, a_{2W}, \ldots, a_{nW})^T \qquad (3.15)$$

where a_{jw} indicates the preference of the criterion j over the worst criterion W. It is clear that $a_{ww} = 1$.

Step 5. Find the optimal weights.

$$(w_1^*, w_2^*, \ldots, w_n^*) \qquad (3.16)$$

The objective is to find the most favorable weights for the criterion, in order to minimize the maximum absolute disparities $\left| \dfrac{W_B}{W_j} - a_{Bj} \right|$ and $\left| \dfrac{W_j}{W_w} - a_{jw} \right|$ for every j, which can be expressed as follows.

  minmax model (Model I):

$$minmax_j \left\{ \left| \frac{w_B}{w_j} - a_{Bj} \right|, \left| \frac{w_j}{w_w} - a_{jw} \right| \right\}$$

$$s.i.$$

$$\sum_j w_j = 1$$

$$w_j \geq 0, \ for \ all \ j \qquad (3.17)$$

Model II

Model (I) is equivalent to the following model (Model II):

$$min \ z$$

$$s.i.$$

$$\left| \frac{w_B}{w_j} - a_{Bj} \right| \leq z, \quad for \ all \ j$$

$$\left| \frac{w_j}{w_w} - a_{jw} \right| \le z, \quad \text{for all } j$$

$$\sum_j w_j = 1$$

$$w_j \ge 0, \quad \text{for all } j \tag{3.18}$$

Solving problem (1), the optimal weights $\left(w_1^*, w_2^*, ..., w_n^*\right)$ and z^* are obtained.

As for minimum consistency $a_{Bj} = a_{jw} = a_{BW}$, and the following formulas are obtained:

$$\left(a_{BW} - z\right) \times \left(a_{BW} - z\right) = \left(a_{BW} + z\right) \Rightarrow z^2 - \left(1 + 2a_{BW}\right)z + \left(a_{BW}^2 - a_{BW}\right) = 0 \tag{3.19}$$

Solving for different values of $a_{BW} \in \{1,2,...,9\}$, the maximum possible z (*max z*) can be found. These maximum values are used as consistency index (see Table 3.3) (Yücel & Taşabat, 2019).

Table 3.3: Consistency Index (CI) Table

a_{BW}	1	2	3	4	5	6	7	8	9
Consistency Index (max z)	0.00	0.44	1.00	1.63	2.30	3.00	3.73	4.47	5.23

Next, the consistency ratio is computed by utilizing the value of z^* and the appropriate consistency index in the following manner:

$$Consistency\ Ratio = \frac{z^*}{Consistency\ Index} \tag{3.20}$$

Consistency Ratio $\in \{0,1\}$, values close to "0" show more consistency, while values close to "1" show less consistency.

3.1.2.3. Equal Weights Method

The equal weights method states all criteria have the same level of importance. "n" standing for the number of available criteria and "l" standing for the sum, all criteria have a weight value of "l/n".

3.1.3. Determining the Measurement Method

One of the steps in the operation of MCDM methods is to perform calculations using the measurement method required by the method under consideration. In MCDM methods, both the measurement method used, and the approach preferred to rank the results can be carried out in different approaches rather than in their original form. These approaches can be generally characterized as modifications.

1. In this case, the measurement method used in the MCDM method under consideration must comply with one of the three cases listed below:
2. Use of the measurement method proposed in traditional (original) methods: In this approach, alternatives are ranked using the measurement method used by the original method.
3. Modification of the measurement method proposed in traditional (original) methods: In this approach, the calculations are performed by modifying the approach used in the original method.

Proposition of a completely different measurement method than those proposed in traditional (original) methods: In this approach, a completely different measurement method is used instead of the measurement method considered in the original method.

3.1.4. Determining the Ranking Method

The final step of MCDM methods is to rank the results. As with the measurement method to be used, different approaches can be used in the ranking method step. These are listed below:

1. Use of the ranking method proposed in traditional (original) methods: In this approach, alternatives are ranked using the ranking method used by the original method.

2. Modification of the ranking method proposed in traditional (original) methods: In this approach, the alternatives are ranked by modifying the approach used in the original method.
3. Proposition of a completely different ranking method than those proposed in traditional (original) methods: This is the use of a completely different ranking method instead of the ranking method considered in the original method.

3.2. Related Studies

The MCDM methods of ELECTRE, TOPSIS, VIKOR, and PROMETHEE are commonly used in decision-making and have been the subject of numerous research studies. These studies have explored various aspects of these methods, including their implementation in different fields, hybridization with other methods, and modification to make them fuzzier. The ranking of countries' development levels is an example of a topic that has been examined using these methods in the book. However, it has been emphasized that different methods or processes can be used while implementing MCDM methods, and the results from traditional methods may vary. These differences, referred to as weaknesses of MCDM methods, have been tested among these four traditional methods, and the traditional methods have been modified accordingly.

Below is the research on rankings of countries' development levels determined by ELECTRE, PROMETHEE, TOPSIS and VIKOR.

Engineer et al. (2008) investigates the implications of using the Human Development Index (HDI) as a benchmark for economic development strategies. They analyze the outcomes of implementing strategies that aim to maximize the Human Development Index (HDI) score for a certain country. In order to accomplish this, the researchers construct an economic framework where a decision-maker determines the allocation of funds to optimize a clearly specified objective function, with the Human Development Index (HDI) being a specific example of such a function. They obtain two main outcomes. Initially, the planner prioritizes the reduction of consumption while simultaneously allocating more resources towards education and health. They accomplish this result even though the HDI includes an income index as one of its components. Furthermore, the optimal strategy typically implies fair distributions, even if the Human Development Index (HDI) does not explicitly address a preference for reducing inequality (Engineer, King, & Roy, 2008).

A new HDI is developed using a multicriteria approach and it is used to rank the Governorates of Egypt (ZeinEldin & Khater, 2013). Safari and Ebrahimi (2014) used the method Modified Similarity Multi-Criteria Decision-making method to rank the countries based on multi-criteria HDI. He used the four indices mentioned in 2010 and 2011 HDRs to rank 187 countries. The results of ranking obtained by the Modified Similarity technique differed from the 2011 HDR ranking. There were some criticisms against HDI's calculation in the form of allocating equal weights to health, education, and income. Therefore, to overcome these weaknesses, Safari created the modified version of the Similarity technique which also has some discrepancies (Safari & Ebrahimi, 2014). The results of the study by Safari and Ebrahimi (2014) showed that different methods and weighting techniques led to different rankings of countries in terms of human development levels. The study found that the results of ranking countries using the Modified Similarity technique may differ from the rankings based on the traditional HDI calculation. Additional, MCDM methods provide a formal approach for ranking alternatives based on various criteria and can be useful for proper ranking of countries in annual human development reports the study also highlight the limitations of the traditional HDI calculation and propose a modified approach that takes into account a broader range of factors and uses MCDM techniques for ranking countries.

In a study conducted by Taşabat and Başer (2017), the human development levels of the countries; EU members, candidates and potential members were examined by using Life Expectancy index, Education index and GNI per capita (PPP $). For this purpose, two Multicriteria Decision-making Methods (MCDM): TOPSIS and WSA were used. These methods were applied by using three weighting techniques; equal weighted, point method and Saaty's method separately. The results obtained were compared with the values of HDI. The results of the study show that the rankings of countries' human development levels vary depending on the MCDM method and weighting technique used. The countries in the "very highly developed" group according to the HDI are also categorized similarly with the results of TOPSIS and WSA methods using equal weighting. However, there are some variations in rankings when using different weighting techniques.

Taşabat 2019 proposed a new MCDM method in which distance, similarity and correlation measures are used. It is called DSC TOPSIS where DSC refers to the initials of distance, similarity and correlation. In this proposed method, for DSC measures, Euclidean, cosine and Pearson correlation was used respectively. The positive and negative values obtained from those measures led to a common positive and negative ideal values respectively. Then DSC TOPSIS is reviewed through standardization and weighting. The study suggested three new ranking index methods by testing the variables that show the development levels of the countries. The results, then were compared to the HDI (Taşabat, 2019).

Taşabat and Özkan (2020) studied the TOPSIS and VIKOR methods as an alternative to the Human Development Index (HDI) calculation made by the United Nations. In order to do that, they discussed about the data set used in HDI. They added the unemployment variable data to this data set consisting of life, income and education variables. To determine the development level of the countries, they used TOPSIS and VIKOR methods. With the ranking of the values obtained, countries were ranked according to their development level. After the sorting of the countries by VIKOR and TOPSIS method separately, spearman rho was calculated for the consistency of rankings obtained. As a result of the examination of this consistency of rankings, it was found that the three methods have a high correlation among each other. They asserted that along with the variables of life, income and education, the unemployment variable can also be used to measure countries' development levels and various methods can be used instead of HDI's calculation method (Taşabat & Özkan, 2020).

Omrani, Alizadeh and Amini's study (2020) uses MULTIMOORA method which differs from the other related studies. They propose a new method for calculating the semi-human development index (HDI) in the provinces of Iran. Their study addresses the limitations of traditional HDI scores and introduces the best worst method (BWM) and multi-objective optimization by ratio analysis (MULTIMOORA) to assess the dimensions of health, education, and living standards. The weights of criteria in each dimension are determined based on policy makers' preferences, and the provinces are ranked accordingly. The findings reveal that Kohgiluyeh & Boyer-Ahmad province is the most developed, while Sistan & Baluchestan province is the least developed. The study provides valuable insights into evaluating development levels and offers a comprehensive approach for policy makers to understand and improve human development in Iran.

Chapter 4   Investigation of the Weaknesses of MCDM Methods

In this section, the four MDCM methods, ELECTRE, PROMETHEE TOPSIS and VIKOR, which were previously explained in Chapter 2, will be modified by addressing one of the weaknesses discussed in Chapter 3. The impact of these modifications, which are aimed at addressing the identified weaknesses, will be discussed. Any method discussed within the scope of the book and described as a weakness can be applied to any MCDM method. If it has the properties described in Section 3.1

The Inequality-adjusted Human Development Index (IHDI) data will be used to demonstrate the working of both traditional and modified versions of the ELECTRE, PROMETHEE TOPSIS and VIKOR MCDM methods. The following sub-sections will provide information about the IHDI data set, followed by the steps and results of both the traditional and modified methods.

4.1. Human Development Index

The Human Development Approach, as developed by Pakistani economist Mahbub ul Haq, aims to improve human life by expanding the richness of human life, rather than focusing solely on economic welfare The Human Development Index (HDI) was introduced by the United Nations in 1990 as a tool to measure and rank countries' levels of social and economic development In 1989, the Human Development Approach was transformed into an index supported by the United Nations Development Program (UNDP, 2023) which was named the HDI (Safari & Ebrahimi, 2014)

HDI summarizes the average achievement of three dimensions of human development—a long and healthy life, access to knowledge and a decent standard of living—by the geometric means of normalized indices of these dimensions.

Figure 4.1. shows the dimensions and indicators of the HDI index (HDI, HDI Dimensions and Indicators, 2023).

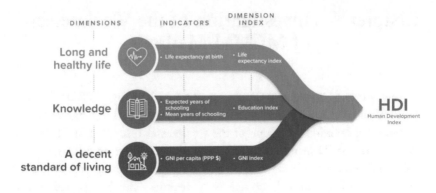

Figure 4.1: The dimensions and indicators of HDI.

4.1.1. Data Sources

- Life expectancy at birth: UNDESA (2019).
- Expected years of schooling: UNESCO Institute for Statistics (2020), ICF Macro Demographic and Health Surveys (2008–2020), United Nations Children's Fund (UNICEF) Multiple Indicator Cluster Surveys (2008–2020) and OECD (2019).
- Mean years of schooling: UNESCO Institute for Statistics (2020), Barro and Lee (2018), ICF Macro Demographic and Health Surveys (2008–2020), UNICEF Multiple Indicator Cluster Surveys (2008–2020) and OECD (2019).
- GNI per capita: World Bank (2020), IMF (2020), United Nations Statistics Division (2020)

4.1.2. Steps to Calculate the Human Development Index

There are two steps to calculating the HDI (HDI, Human Development Index Technical Notes, 2022):

Step 1. Creating the dimension indices

Goalposts, representing the minimum and maximum values, are established to convert indicators, which are stated in various units, into indices ranging from 0 to 1. The goalposts serve as the reference points for both the minimum and maximum values, known as the "natural zeros" and "aspirational targets" respectively, against which the component indicators are standardized. This is illustrated in Equation 4.1 below. The values are set as indicated in Table 4.1.

Table 4.1: Minimum and Maximum Values

Dimension	Indicator	Minimum	Maximum
Health	Life expectancy (years)	20	85
Education	Expected years of schooling (years)	0	18
	Mean years of schooling (years)	0	15
Standard of living	GNI per capita (2017 PPP$)	100	75,000

Based on historical data demonstrating that no country in the twentieth century had a life expectancy of less than 20 years, the natural zero for life expectancy is 20 years (Śleszyński, 2016).

The decision was made to establish the maximum life expectancy at 85 years old, which seems to be a feasible goal given the ongoing improvement in people's living conditions and medical advancements. For instance, the life expectancy in Japan is 84.5 years and in Hong Kong, China (SAR), it is 84.7 years.

Because society can survive without education, the minimum is placed at 0. The predicted maximum year of education is set at 18 years since, in the majority of nations, this is the total time required to earn a master's degree. The maximum mean for education is set at 15 years as a guide for 2025.

With respect to the challenges assessing subsistence and nonmarket output in nations with low GNIs, $100 is defined as the minimal gross national income (GNI) per capita. $75,000 is the maximum per person. However, Kahneman and Deaton (2010) assert that levels of annual income per capita over $75,000 have no impact on human development and well-being.

$$Dimension\ index = \frac{actual\ value - minimum\ value}{maximum\ value - minimum\ value} \qquad (4.1)$$

With regard to the education dimension, equation 1 is first applied to the indicators for each one of them, and then the arithmetic mean of the two resulting indices is calculated. This means that the mean and expected years of schooling are equivalent because adults in developing countries have lower levels of education compared to school-age children, but they are willing to achieve universal primary and secondary enrollment.

According to Anand and Sen (2010), the translation function from revenue to capabilities is probably concave, meaning that increasing revenue has little effect on capability growth. This is thus because each dimension index acts as a decision-making agent for the corresponding dimension. As a result, the income is calculated using the natural logarithm of the actual, minimum, and maximum values.

Step 2. Aggregating the dimensional indices to produce the Human Development Index

The HDI is the geometric mean of the three-dimensional indices (Equation 4.2):

$$HDI = \left(I_{Health} \cdot I_{Education} \cdot I_{Income} \right)^{1/3} \tag{4.2}$$

Calculation of HDI value for Guyana is shown in Table 4.2

Example 4.1: Guyana

Table 4.2: Calculation of Guyana HDI Value

Indicator	Value
Life expectancy at birth (years)	65.7
Expected years of schooling (years)	12.5
Mean years of schooling (years)	8.6
Gross national income per capita (2017 PPP $)	22,465

Note: Values are rounded

$$Health\,Index = \frac{65.7 - 20}{85 - 20} = 0.703$$

$$Expected\,years\,of\,schooling\,index = \frac{12.5 - 0}{18 - 0} = 0.694$$

$$Mean\ years\ of\ schooling\ index = \frac{8.6 - 0}{15 - 0} = 0.573$$

$$Education\ index = \frac{0.694 + 0.573}{2} = 0.634$$

$$Income\ index = \frac{\ln(22,465) - \ln(100)}{\ln(75,000) - \ln(100)} = 0.818$$

$$Human\ Development\ Index = (0.703 * 0.634 * 0.818)^{1/3} = 0.714$$

4.1.3. Methodology Used to Express Income

The World Bank's 2022 World Development Indicators database contains GNI per capita estimates for several nations, presented in constant 2017 purchasing power parity (PPP) levels. The Human Development Report Office (HDRO) employs a two-step procedure to convert GNI per capita in local currency from current to constant terms in cases when nations have incomplete or missing data for this indicator. The GNI per capita in current dollars is initially converted into PPP dollars for the base year 2017. The second phase is incorporating the actual growth rates into the GNI per capita in PPP terms for the reference year, resulting in a chronological sequence of GNI per capita in constant 2017 PPP terms. The actual rates of economic growth for countries are determined by the correlation between the nominal growth of Gross National Income (GNI) per person in local currency and the GDP deflator. In cases where countries lack a GNI per capita value in constant 2017 PPP terms for 2021 as reported in the World Development Indicators (WDI) database, the most recent GNI values in constant PPT terms are determined using the available real growth rates of GDP per capita from either the WDI's database or the International Monetary Fund's World Economic Outlook database.

The International Comparison Program (ICP) generates the official purchasing power parity (PPP) conversion rates by conducting regular surveys that gather price data for comparable commodities and services across multiple nations.

The last one refers to 2017, having collected data from 176 countries.

4.1.4. Estimating Missing Values

For a few countries which miss one of the four indicators, the HDRO made estimations based on cross country regression models.

This research predicted expected years of schooling for the Bahamas, Dominica, Equatorial Guinea, Haiti, Libya, Papua New Guinea, Tonga, Trinidad and Tobago, and Vanuatu, as well as mean years of schooling for Eritrea, Grenada, and Saint Kitts and Nevis.

4.1.5. Human Development Categories

The 2014 Human Development Report established specified cutoff lines for four types of human development outcomes. The cutoff points (COP) are the HDI values obtained using the quartiles (q) from the distributions of the component indicators averaged between 2004 and 2013:

$$COP_q = HDI\left(LE_q, EYS_q, MYS_q, GNIpc_q\right), q = 1, 2, 3. \qquad (4.3)$$

For example, LE1, LE2, and LE3 represent three quartiles of the distribution of life expectancy among countries. This report maintains the same HDI cutoff parameters for categorizing nations that were introduced in the 2014 report.

Table 4.3: Cutoff Points of the HDI for Grouping Countries

Categories	Cutoff points
Very high human development	0.800 and above
High human development	0.700.799
Medium human development	0.550.699
Low human development	Below 0.550

4.1.6. Human Development Index Aggregates

Applying the HDI formula to the weighted group averages of component indicators results in the calculation of the aggregate HDI values for country groupings (human development category, region, etc.). The weights for the whole population, the population aged 5 to 24, and the population aged

25 and older are the life expectancy, the gross national income (GNI) per capita, the projected years of schooling, and the mean years of schooling.

4.2. Inequality-Adjusted Human Development Index

The Inequality-Adjusted Human Development Index (IHDI) (HDI, Human Development Index Technical Notes, 2022) combines a country's average successes in health, education, and income with how those achievements are divided among the population by "discounting" each dimension's average value in accordance with its degree of inequality (IHDI, 2023). That means, The IHDI is distribution-sensitive rather than association-sensitive. Therefore, the two countries may have different distributions of achievements while having the same average HDI value. The IHDI and HDI must be equal for there to be perfect equality; but, as inequality rises, the IHDI falls below the HDI.

The IHDI and HDI differ from each other in terms of human development cost of inequality, meaning inequality being the reason for the overall loss to human development. The IHDI shows a direct link to inequalities in dimensions, may contribute to the policies to decrease inequality and provides a better understanding of inequalities and their contribution to the overall human development cost. The coefficient of human equality, introduced in 2014 as an experimental measure, is calculated as an unweighted average of inequality across education, health and income.

According to 2021 data the IHDI is calculated for 156 countries.

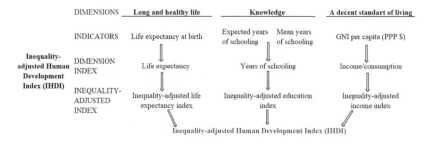

Figure 4.2: Inequality-adjusted Human Development Index (IHDI).
Source: (HDI, Human Development Index Technical Notes, 2022).

The IHDI is used to adjust the HDI for inequality in the distribution of each dimension within the population. It is distribution- sensitive indices of human development suggested by Foster, (Foster, Lopez-Calva, & Szekely, 2005), drawing on the Atkinson (1970) family of inequality measures. Calculated as the geometric mean of inequality-adjusted dimensional indices, the IHDI explains these inequalities by "discounting" each dimension's average value in accordance with its level of inequality. Since the IHDI falls below the HDI when inequality increases, it can be seen that the IHDI calculates the level of human development when inequality is explained.

4.2.1. Data Sources

In order to gain a comprehensive understanding of the distribution of each dimension across the population, the IHDI needs to utilize supplementary data sources. This is necessary because the HDI primarily depends on country-level averages, such as national accounts, to measure income. The distributions are observed using distinct units. Life expectancy is categorized based on a hypothetical group of people, whereas years of schooling and income are categorized based on individual people

Inequality in the distribution of HDI dimensions is estimated for (HDI, Human Development Index Technical Notes, 2022):

Life expectancy, using data from complete life tables provided by UNDESA (2022a). Mortality rates and other statistics are given for each age group (0, 1, 2, 3, ... 100+).

Mean years of schooling, using household surveys data harmonized in international databases, including the Luxembourg Income Study, Eurostat's European Union Survey of Income and Living Conditions, the World Bank's International Income Distribution Database, ICF Macro's Demographic and Health Surveys, United Nations Children's Fund's Multiple Indicators Cluster Surveys, the Center for Distributive, Labor and Social Studies and the World Bank's Socio Economic Database for Latin America and the Caribbean, the United Nations Educational, Scientific and Cultural Organization Institute for Statistics' Educational Attainment Table and the United Nations University's World Income Inequality Database.

Databases and household surveys are used to calculate disposable household income or consumption per capita. In some countries, income is imputed using asset index matching from household surveys (Harttgen & Vollmer, 2013). The asset index is based on microdata from the ICF Macro Demographic and Health

Surveys and the United Nations Children's Fund Multiple Indicator Cluster surveys (HDI, Human Development Index Technical Notes, 2022)

4.2.2. Steps to Calculate the Inequality-adjusted Human Development Index

There are three steps to calculating the IHDI.

Step 1. Estimating inequality in the dimensions of the Human Development Index

The Inequality-Adjusted Human Development Index (IHDI) is calculated using Atkinson's (1970) inequality measures, with a specific aversion parameter value of 4.4. The inequality aversion parameter determines the extent to which lesser accomplishments are given more importance while greater achievements are given less importance. The inequality measure for this case may be calculated using the formula $A = 1 - \frac{g}{\mu}$, where g represents the geometric mean and μ represents the arithmetic mean of the distribution. The expression for this can be represented as:

$$A_x = 1 - \frac{\sqrt[n]{X_1 \ldots X_n}}{\underline{X}} \qquad (4.4)$$

where $\{X_1, \ldots, X_n\}$ represents the distribution in the specific dimension being considered. A_x is calculated for each variable (life expectancy, mean years of schooling, and disposable family income or consumption per capita). Zero values are not permitted in equation 4.4 when calculating the geometric mean. To calculate the inequality, the mean years of education are used as a baseline, and one year is added to all valid observations. To calculate income per capita, all negative or zero incomes, as well as incomes in the bottom 0.5 percentile, are replaced with the minimum value of the second bottom 0.5 percentile of the positive income distribution. To mitigate the influence of measurement mistakes when reporting extremely high wages, the upper 0.5 percentile of the distribution is truncated. Kovacevic (2010/33) conducts a sensitivity analysis of the Inequality-Adjusted Human Development Index (IHDI).

Step 2. Adjusting the dimension indices for inequality

The inequality-adjusted dimension indices are obtained from the HDI dimension indices, I_x, by multiplying them by $(1 - A_x)$, where A_x, defined by equation 1, is the corresponding Atkinson measure:

$$I_x^* = 1 - A_x . I_x$$

$$I_x^* = (1 - A_x) . I_x \qquad (4.5)$$

The inequality-adjusted income index, denoted as I^* is derived from the index of logarithmically transformed income values, denoted as I inc. The inequality-adjusted income index, denoted as I^* is calculated using the logarithm of income values (I income*) and takes into account income inequality in the distribution of income, which is derived using income at different levels. This allows the IHDI to consider the complete impact of income inequality.

Step 3. Combining the dimension indices to calculate the Inequality-adjusted Human Development Index

The IHDI is the geometric mean of the three-dimension indices adjusted for inequality (Equation 4.6):

$$IHDI = \left(I_{Health}^* . I_{Education}^* . I_{Income}^* \right)^{1/3}$$

$$= \left[(1 - A_{Health}) . (1 - A_{Education}) . (1 - A_{Income}) \right]^{1/3} . HDI \qquad (4.6)$$

The loss in the HDI value due to inequality is (Equation 4.7):

$$Loss = 1 - \left[(1 - A_{Health}) . (1 - A_{Education}) . (1 - A_{Income}) \right]^{1/3} \qquad (4.7)$$

4.2.3. Coefficient of Human Inequality

The coefficient of human inequality is a measure that represents the unweighted average of disparities in health, education, and income. It calculates the average of these inequalities using the arithmetic mean (Equation 4.8):

$$Coefficient\ of\ human\ inequality = \frac{A_{Health} + A_{Education} + A_{Income}}{3} \qquad (4.8)$$

When the differences in dimensions are similar in size, the coefficient of human inequality and the decrease in HDI value only experience minimal changes. When there are differences in the extent of inequalities, the decrease in HDI value tends to exceed the coefficient of human inequality.

4.2.4. Notes on Methodology and Caveats

The Atkinson index, which satisfies the subgroup consistency, is used by the IHDI. This characteristic ensures that changes in the distribution of human development within a particular segment of the population will correspond to changes in the distribution throughout the entire population. The IHDI's fundamental flaw is that it lacks association sensitivity, which makes it impossible to precisely explain overlapping disparities. All of the data for each person must be available from a single survey source in order for the measure association to be sensitive, which is currently unlikely for the majority of nations.

Calculation of Kazakhstan HDI and IHDI values is given Table 4.4

Example 4.2: Kazakhstan

Table 4.4: Calculation of Kazakhstan HDI and IHDI Values

Indicator	Value	Dimension index	Inequality measure (A)[a]	Inequality-adjusted index (I*)
Life expectancy (years)	69.4	0.7594	0.073	(0.073).0.7594=0.7042
Expected years of schooling (years)	15.8	0.8758	-	-
Mean years of schooling (years)	12.3	0.8232	0.032	-
Education index		0.8495	0.032	(1–0.032). 0.8495=0.8226
Gross national income per capita (2017 PPP $)	23,943	0.8275	0.103	(1–0.103).0.8275=0.742

(*continued*)

Table 4.4:   Continued

Indicator	Value	Dimension index	Inequality measure (A)[a]	Inequality-adjusted index (I^{*})
Human Development Index		Inequality-adjusted Human Development Index		
$(0.7594.0.8495.0.8275)^{1/2} = 0.811$		$(0.7042. 0.8226. 0.742)^{1/2} = 0.755$		
Loss due to inequality (%):		Coefficient of human inequality (%)		
$100.\left(1 - \dfrac{0.755}{0.811}\right) = 6.9$		$\dfrac{100.(0.073 + 0.032 + 0.103)}{3} = 6.9$		

Note: Values are rounded. a. Inequalities are estimated from micro data.

In line with the above calculations, the values obtained for some world countries are shown in Table 4.5. The remaining data can be found in HDR21-22_Statistical_Annex_I-HDI_Table.xlsx (live.com)

Table 4.5: Inequality-adjusted HDI Data (2021)[1]

HDI rank	Country	HDI Value 2021	IHDI Value 2021	IHDI Overall loss (%) 2021	Difference from HDI rank 2021	Coefficient of human inequality (%) 2021	Inequality in life expectancy (%) 2021	Inequality-adjusted life expectancy index Value 2021	Inequality in education (%) 2021	Inequality-adjusted education index Value 2021	Inequality in income (%) 2021	Inequality-adjusted income index Value 2021	Income shares held by (%) Poorest 40% 2010–2021	Income shares held by (%) Richest 10% 2010–2021	Income shares held by (%) Richest 1% 2021	Gini coefficient 2010–2021
	Very high human development															
1	Switzerland	0,962	0,894	7,1	-3	6,9	3,1	0,954	2,0	0,902	15,6	0,830	19,9	25,8	11,5	33,1
2	Norway	0,961	0,908	5,5	0	5,4	2,5	0,948	2,3	0,912	11,4	0,866	22,9	22,4	8,9	27,7
3	Iceland	0,959	0,915	4,6	2	4,6	2,0	0,945	2,2	0,938	9,5	0,864	23,9	22,1	8,8	26,1
4	Hong Kong, China (SAR)	0,952	0,828	13,0	-19	12,4	2,1	0,979	9,7	0,802	25,6	0,724	..	..	17,9	..
5	Australia	0,951	0,876	7,9	-6	7,6	2,7	0,966	3,1	0,896	17,1	0,776	19,5	26,6	11,3	34,3
6	Denmark	0,948	0,898	5,3	3	5,2	3,0	0,916	2,5	0,909	10,1	0,870	23,5	23,5	12,9	27,7
7	Sweden	0,947	0,885	6,5	0	6,4	2,6	0,944	3,9	0,885	12,8	0,830	21,9	22,7	10,5	29,3
8	Ireland	0,945	0,886	6,2	2	6,2	2,8	0,927	3,4	0,856	12,3	0,877	21,8	25,1	11,8	30,6
9	Germany	0,942	0,883	6,3	1	6,2	3,4	0,901	2,7	0,917	12,5	0,833	20,8	25,1	12,8	31,7
10	Netherlands	0,941	0,878	6,7	1	6,7	3,3	0,917	4,9	0,875	11,9	0,842	22,3	23,9	6,9	29,2

1 HDR21-22_Statistical_Annex_I-HDI_Table.xlsx (live.com)

The definition of the headings in Table 4.5 is as follows.[2]

"Human Development Index (HDI): A composite index measuring average achievement in three basic dimensions of human development—a long and healthy life, knowledge and a decent standard of living. See Technical note 1 at hdr2021-22_technical_notes.pdf (undp.org) for details on how the HDI is calculated.

Inequality-adjusted HDI (IHDI): HDI value adjusted for inequalities in the three basic dimensions of human development. See Technical note 2 at hdr2021-22_technical_notes.pdf (undp.org) for details on how the IHDI is calculated.

Coefficient of human inequality: Average inequality in the three basic dimensions of human development.

Inequality in life expectancy: Inequality in distribution of expected length of life based on data from life tables estimated using the Atkinson inequality index.

Inequality-adjusted life expectancy index: HDI life expectancy index value adjusted for inequality in distribution of expected length of life based on data from life tables listed in Main data sources.

Inequality in education: Inequality in distribution of years of schooling based on data from household surveys estimated using the Atkinson inequality index.

Inequality-adjusted education index: HDI education index value adjusted for inequality in distribution of years of schooling based on data from household surveys listed in Main data sources.

Inequality in income: Inequality in income distribution based on data from household surveys estimated using the Atkinson inequality index.

Inequality-adjusted income index: HDI income index value adjusted for inequality in income distribution based on data from household surveys listed in Main data sources.

Income shares: Percentage share of income (or consumption) that accrues to the indicated population subgroups.

Income share held by richest 1 %: Share of pretax national income held by the richest 1% of the population. Pretax national income is the sum

---

*of all pretax personal income flows accruing to the owners of the pro-
duction factors, labor and capital before the tax/transfer system is taken
into account and after the pension system is taken into account.*
Overall loss: *Percentage difference between the IHDI value and the
HDI value.*
Difference from HDI rank: *Difference in ranks on the IHDI and the HDI,
calculated only for countries for which an IHDI value is calculated.*
Gini coefficient: *Measure of the deviation of the distribution of income
among individuals or households in a country from a perfectly equal
distribution. A value of 0 represents absolute equality, a value of 100
absolute inequality."*

According to the cut-off points of the HDI for grouping countries that were
previously mentioned in Table 4.3 were shown in the table above.

Countries without an IHDI value are shown in Table 4.6 (HDR21-22_
Statistical_Annex_I-HDI_Table.xlsx (live.com)).

Table 4.6: Countries Without an IHDI Value (2021)

HDI rank	Country	Human Development Index (HDI)	Inequality-adjusted HDI (IHDI)	Inequality-adjusted life expectancy index	Inequality-adjusted education index	Inequality-adjusted income index
16	Liechtenstein	0,935	..	0,927	..	..
26	United Arab Emirates	0,911	..	0,862	0,751	..
35	Bahrain	0,875	..	0,863	0,718	..
35	Saudi Arabia	0,875	..	0,831	0,676	..
40	Andorra	0,858	..	0,880	0,649	..
42	Qatar	0,855	..	0,877	0,607	..
44	San Marino	0,853	..	0,910	0,662	..
50	Kuwait	0,831	..	0,853	0,522	..
51	Brunei Darussalam	0,829	..	0,778	..	..
55	Bahamas	0,812	..	0,724	0,726	..
57	Trinidad and Tobago	0,810	..	0,726	..	..
62	Malaysia	0,803	..	0,794	0,638	..
68	Grenada	0,795	..	0,764	..	..

(continued)

Table 4.6:   Continued

HDI rank	Country	Human Development Index (HDI)	Inequality-adjusted HDI (IHDI)	Inequality-adjusted life expectancy index	Inequality-adjusted education index	Inequality-adjusted income index
71	Antigua and Barbuda	0,788	..	0,857	..	..
75	Saint Kitts and Nevis	0,777	..	0,732	..	..
80	Palau	0,767	..	0,620	0,836	..
83	Cuba	0,764	..	0,788	0,743	..
89	Saint Vincent and the Grenadines	0,751	..	0,694	0,698	..
99	Fiji	0,730	..	0,614	0,753	..
101	Uzbekistan	0,727	..	0,716	0,739	..
102	Dominica	0,720	..	0,740	..	..
104	Libya	0,718	..	0,736	..	..
112	Lebanon	0,706	..	0,800	0,567	..
117	Botswana	0,693	..	0,496	0,526	..
128	Cabo Verde	0,662	..	0,758	0,405	..
131	Marshall Islands	0,639	..	0,575	0,616	..
134	Micronesia (Federated States of)	0,628	..	0,672	..	0,401
140	Vanuatu	0,607	..	0,667	..	0,416
145	Equatorial Guinea	0,596	..	0,437	..	..
149	Myanmar	0,585	..	0,554	0,377	..
150	Syrian Arab Republic	0,577	..	0,697	..	..
155	Solomon Islands	0,564	..	0,681	..	..
171	Djibouti	0,509	..	0,484	..	0,428
176	Eritrea	0,492	..	0,571	..	..
180	Afghanistan	0,478	..	0,477	0,210	..
..	Korea (Democratic People's Rep. of)	..	..	0,730	..	..
..	Monaco	..	..	0,966	..	..
..	Nauru	..	..	0,581	..	..
..	Somalia	..	..	0,335	..	0,265

Of 195 (191 + 4 others) countries, the values for 39 of them were not calculated, so the IHDI index could be calculated for 156 countries.

In the application of the formulas, 156 countries will be considered. The values were shown in Table 4.7 below.

Table 4.7: Countries Whose IHDI Values Were Calculated (2021).

HDI rank	Country	Human Development Index (HDI)	Inequality-adjusted HDI (IHDI)	Inequality-adjusted life expectancy index	Inequality-adjusted education index	Inequality-adjusted income index
1	Switzerland	0,962	0,894	0,954	0,902	0,830
2	Norway	0,961	0,908	0,948	0,912	0,866
3	Iceland	0,959	0,915	0,945	0,938	0,864
4	Hong Kong, China (SAR)	0,952	0,828	0,979	0,802	0,724
5	Australia	0,951	0,876	0,966	0,896	0,776
6	Denmark	0,948	0,898	0,916	0,909	0,870
7	Sweden	0,947	0,885	0,944	0,885	0,830
8	Ireland	0,945	0,886	0,927	0,856	0,877
9	Germany	0,942	0,883	0,901	0,917	0,833
10	Netherlands	0,941	0,878	0,917	0,875	0,842
11	Finland	0,940	0,890	0,928	0,907	0,839
12	Singapore	0,939	0,817	0,944	0,771	0,750
13	Belgium	0,937	0,874	0,918	0,859	0,848
13	New Zealand	0,937	0,865	0,921	0,914	0,768
15	Canada	0,936	0,860	0,924	0,893	0,770
17	Luxembourg	0,930	0,850	0,926	0,794	0,833
18	United Kingdom	0,929	0,850	0,898	0,901	0,758
19	Japan	0,925	0,850	0,972	0,829	0,761
19	Korea (Republic of)	0,925	0,838	0,952	0,799	0,773
21	United States	0,921	0,819	0,828	0,883	0,751
22	Israel	0,919	0,815	0,927	0,835	0,700
23	Slovenia	0,918	0,878	0,908	0,898	0,829
23	Malta	0,918	0,849	0,950	0,829	0,776
25	Austria	0,916	0,851	0,917	0,832	0,808
27	Spain	0,905	0,788	0,941	0,717	0,725
28	France	0,903	0,825	0,925	0,762	0,797

(continued)

Table 4.7:   Continued

HDI rank	Country	Human Development Index (HDI)	Inequality-adjusted HDI (IHDI)	Inequality-adjusted life expectancy index	Inequality-adjusted education index	Inequality-adjusted income index
29	Cyprus	0,896	0,819	0,917	0,768	0,781
30	Italy	0,895	0,791	0,940	0,727	0,724
31	Estonia	0,890	0,829	0,853	0,876	0,763
32	Czechia	0,889	0,850	0,860	0,868	0,821
33	Greece	0,887	0,791	0,891	0,777	0,714
34	Poland	0,876	0,816	0,834	0,845	0,770
35	Lithuania	0,875	0,800	0,791	0,870	0,744
38	Portugal	0,866	0,773	0,909	0,685	0,741
39	Latvia	0,863	0,792	0,790	0,872	0,722
40	Croatia	0,858	0,797	0,853	0,791	0,751
42	Chile	0,855	0,722	0,862	0,732	0,596
45	Slovakia	0,848	0,803	0,805	0,819	0,787
46	Hungary	0,846	0,792	0,806	0,802	0,767
47	Argentina	0,842	0,720	0,787	0,818	0,580
48	Türkiye	0,838	0,717	0,811	0,680	0,667
49	Montenegro	0,832	0,756	0,847	0,760	0,670
52	Russian Federation	0,822	0,751	0,718	0,846	0,697
53	Romania	0,821	0,733	0,793	0,729	0,682
54	Oman	0,816	0,708	0,751	0,698	0,676
56	Kazakhstan	0,811	0,755	0,704	0,823	0,742
58	Uruguay	0,809	0,710	0,807	0,717	0,619
58	Costa Rica	0,809	0,664	0,826	0,666	0,533
60	Belarus	0,808	0,765	0,780	0,803	0,715
61	Panama	0,805	0,640	0,771	0,633	0,536
63	Serbia	0,802	0,720	0,799	0,723	0,647
63	Georgia	0,802	0,706	0,743	0,836	0,566
63	Mauritius	0,802	0,666	0,736	0,601	0,667
66	Thailand	0,800	0,686	0,841	0,608	0,630
67	Albania	0,796	0,710	0,810	0,682	0,649
68	Bulgaria	0,795	0,701	0,756	0,721	0,633
70	Barbados	0,790	0,657	0,815	0,722	0,483
72	Seychelles	0,785	0,661	0,715	0,681	0,593
73	Sri Lanka	0,782	0,676	0,823	0,663	0,567
74	Bosnia and Herzegovina	0,780	0,677	0,817	0,626	0,606

Table 4.7:   Continued

HDI rank	Country	Human Development Index (HDI)	Inequality-adjusted HDI (IHDI)	Inequality-adjusted life expectancy index	Inequality-adjusted education index	Inequality-adjusted income index
76	Iran (Islamic Republic of)	0,774	0,686	0,758	0,723	0,590
77	Ukraine	0,773	0,726	0,748	0,758	0,675
78	North Macedonia	0,770	0,686	0,792	0,659	0,619
79	China	0,768	0,651	0,848	0,573	0,567
80	Moldova (Republic of)	0,767	0,711	0,685	0,775	0,677
80	Dominican Republic	0,767	0,618	0,667	0,605	0,583
84	Peru	0,762	0,635	0,736	0,649	0,535
85	Armenia	0,759	0,688	0,744	0,720	0,609
86	Mexico	0,758	0,621	0,699	0,623	0,550
87	Brazil	0,754	0,576	0,730	0,594	0,440
88	Colombia	0,752	0,589	0,737	0,595	0,468
90	Maldives	0,747	0,594	0,884	0,421	0,565
91	Azerbaijan	0,745	0,685	0,673	0,700	0,683
91	Tonga	0,745	0,666	0,716	0,790	0,522
91	Turkmenistan	0,745	0,619	0,607	0,720	0,543
91	Algeria	0,745	0,598	0,760	0,451	0,626
95	Ecuador	0,740	0,604	0,752	0,606	0,483
96	Mongolia	0,739	0,644	0,711	0,643	0,585
97	Tunisia	0,731	0,588	0,745	0,469	0,581
97	Egypt	0,731	0,519	0,690	0,443	0,457
99	Suriname	0,730	0,532	0,688	0,562	0,390
102	Jordan	0,720	0,617	0,757	0,545	0,570
105	Paraguay	0,717	0,582	0,685	0,570	0,506
106	Palestine, State of	0,715	0,584	0,738	0,625	0,432
106	Saint Lucia	0,715	0,559	0,713	0,467	0,525
108	Guyana	0,714	0,591	0,592	0,568	0,613
109	South Africa	0,713	0,471	0,529	0,627	0,316
110	Jamaica	0,709	0,591	0,709	0,633	0,461
111	Samoa	0,707	0,613	0,727	0,674	0,469
112	Gabon	0,706	0,554	0,566	0,517	0,583

(*continued*)

Table 4.7:   Continued

HDI rank	Country	Human Development Index (HDI)	Inequality-adjusted HDI (IHDI)	Inequality-adjusted life expectancy index	Inequality-adjusted education index	Inequality-adjusted income index
114	Indonesia	0,705	0,585	0,635	0,552	0,572
115	Viet Nam	0,703	0,602	0,717	0,541	0,563
116	Philippines	0,699	0,574	0,649	0,597	0,488
118	Kyrgyzstan	0,692	0,627	0,688	0,721	0,497
118	Bolivia (Plurinational State of)	0,692	0,549	0,550	0,620	0,486
120	Venezuela (Bolivarian Republic of)	0,691	0,592	0,678	0,663	0,462
121	Iraq	0,686	0,554	0,667	0,421	0,607
122	Tajikistan	0,685	0,599	0,663	0,659	0,493
123	Belize	0,683	0,535	0,705	0,559	0,389
123	Morocco	0,683	0,504	0,741	0,343	0,502
125	El Salvador	0,675	0,548	0,706	0,450	0,517
126	Nicaragua	0,667	0,516	0,747	0,437	0,422
127	Bhutan	0,666	0,471	0,678	0,279	0,550
129	Bangladesh	0,661	0,503	0,681	0,371	0,504
130	Tuvalu	0,641	0,541	0,587	0,557	0,483
132	India	0,633	0,475	0,604	0,348	0,510
133	Ghana	0,632	0,458	0,520	0,397	0,464
135	Guatemala	0,627	0,460	0,652	0,314	0,475
136	Kiribati	0,624	0,516	0,566	0,537	0,451
137	Honduras	0,621	0,479	0,693	0,406	0,390
138	Sao Tome and Principe	0,618	0,503	0,656	0,470	0,412
139	Namibia	0,615	0,402	0,484	0,428	0,313
140	Lao People's Democratic Republic	0,607	0,459	0,587	0,316	0,521
140	Timor-Leste	0,607	0,440	0,586	0,293	0,496
143	Nepal	0,602	0,449	0,630	0,311	0,462
144	Eswatini (Kingdom of)	0,597	0,424	0,435	0,431	0,407
146	Cambodia	0,593	0,479	0,646	0,355	0,480
146	Zimbabwe	0,593	0,458	0,459	0,535	0,392
148	Angola	0,586	0,407	0,460	0,341	0,430

Table 4.7:   Continued

HDI rank	Country	Human Development Index (HDI)	Inequality-adjusted HDI (IHDI)	Inequality-adjusted life expectancy index	Inequality-adjusted education index	Inequality-adjusted income index
151	Cameroon	0,576	0,393	0,444	0,389	0,352
152	Kenya	0,575	0,426	0,503	0,400	0,384
153	Congo	0,571	0,432	0,529	0,433	0,351
154	Zambia	0,565	0,390	0,475	0,432	0,289
156	Papua New Guinea	0,558	0,397	0,552	0,287	0,396
156	Comoros	0,558	0,310	0,497	0,262	0,229
158	Mauritania	0,556	0,389	0,507	0,238	0,490
159	Côte d'Ivoire	0,550	0,358	0,414	0,256	0,436
160	Tanzania (United Republic of)	0,549	0,418	0,556	0,342	0,385
161	Pakistan	0,544	0,380	0,518	0,221	0,479
162	Togo	0,539	0,372	0,463	0,328	0,340
163	Nigeria	0,535	0,341	0,304	0,310	0,421
163	Haiti	0,535	0,327	0,488	0,285	0,251
165	Rwanda	0,534	0,402	0,571	0,334	0,340
166	Uganda	0,525	0,396	0,523	0,341	0,350
166	Benin	0,525	0,334	0,413	0,249	0,363
168	Lesotho	0,514	0,372	0,341	0,430	0,351
169	Malawi	0,512	0,377	0,530	0,361	0,279
170	Senegal	0,511	0,354	0,593	0,183	0,406
172	Sudan	0,508	0,336	0,522	0,200	0,362
173	Madagascar	0,501	0,367	0,522	0,320	0,295
174	Gambia	0,500	0,348	0,496	0,221	0,384
175	Ethiopia	0,498	0,363	0,532	0,214	0,420
177	Guinea-Bissau	0,483	0,306	0,430	0,240	0,277
178	Liberia	0,481	0,330	0,438	0,266	0,310
179	Congo (Democratic Republic of the)	0,479	0,341	0,412	0,371	0,260
181	Sierra Leone	0,477	0,309	0,400	0,220	0,337
182	Guinea	0,465	0,299	0,389	0,172	0,399
183	Yemen	0,455	0,307	0,493	0,194	0,304

(continued)

Table 4.7:   Continued

HDI rank	Country	Human Development Index (HDI)	Inequality-adjusted HDI (IHDI)	Inequality-adjusted life expectancy index	Inequality-adjusted education index	Inequality-adjusted income index
184	Burkina Faso	0,449	0,315	0,415	0,197	0,381
185	Mozambique	0,446	0,300	0,434	0,232	0,269
186	Mali	0,428	0,291	0,403	0,159	0,386
187	Burundi	0,426	0,302	0,477	0,243	0,238
188	Central African Republic	0,404	0,240	0,334	0,238	0,174
189	Niger	0,400	0,292	0,456	0,172	0,318
190	Chad	0,394	0,251	0,307	0,176	0,290
191	South Sudan	0,385	0,245	0,339	0,208	0,209

4.3. Survey on Weaknesses of MCDM Methods

In the following sub-sections, for ELECTRE III, PROMETHEE TOPSIS and VIKOR and methods, the weaknesses mentioned below will be examined in the data set. For these methods, it is also possible to examine their different weaknesses.

All applications were conducted using Python programming language. Python, a high-level programming language created in the late 1980s, is celebrated for its simplicity and versatility. It emphasizes readability and ease of use, making it a preferred choice for beginners and experienced developers alike. Python's extensive libraries and frameworks support diverse applications, from web development and data analysis to artificial intelligence and automation, solidifying its position as one of the most popular programming languages in the world. Python's clean and readable syntax allows data scientists and optimization professionals to express complex ideas and algorithms in a straightforward manner. This simplicity reduces the learning curve for new users and facilitates code collaboration. Python's popularity has led to a large and active community of developers and experts. This means there are abundant tutorials, documentation, and community forums available to help data scientists and optimization professionals solve problems and learn new techniques (Mastrodomenico, 2022). With regard to the aforementioned aspects of python's ease of usage and the large number of available examples and tutorials, applications of this book were provided in python.

Mainly, **pyDecision**, **NumPy** and **pandas** python libraries were used.

Pandas is a powerful and widely used open-source Python library for data manipulation and analysis. It provides data structures and functions that make working with structured data, such as spreadsheets or databases, more accessible and efficient. Here are some of the core functionalities of the Pandas package:

1. **Data Structures:** Pandas introduces two primary data structures: "DataFrame" and "Series".
   - DataFrame: A two-dimensional, tabular data structure, similar to a spreadsheet or SQL table, where data is organized in rows and columns.
   - Series: A one-dimensional array-like object that can hold data of various types.
2. **Data Import and Export:** Pandas can read data from a wide range of file formats, including CSV, Excel, SQL databases, JSON, and more. It also provides methods for exporting data to these formats.
3. **Data Cleaning and Preprocessing:** Pandas offers functions to handle missing data, remove duplicates, and reformat data. It can handle data cleansing tasks like filling in missing values, removing outliers, and transforming data.
4. **Data Selection and Indexing:** Pandas provides versatile ways to select and filter data based on criteria. You can index, slice, and filter data easily using column names, row labels, or conditions.
5. **Data Transformation:** You can perform operations on data, such as aggregation, sorting, grouping, and reshaping. Pandas enable pivoting, melting, and other transformations to make data suitable for analysis.
6. **Merging and Joining Data:** Pandas can merge multiple data sources based on common columns or keys. This is especially useful when dealing with relational data.
7. **Time Series Data Handling:** Pandas has excellent support for working with time series data, making it suitable for financial and temporal analysis. It can resample data, create date-based indexes, and handle time zones.
8. **Statistical Analysis:** You can perform various statistical calculations and summary statistics on your data, such as mean, median, standard

deviation, and correlation. Pandas also support rolling and exponential moving statistics for time series data.

Pandas is widely used in data science, data analysis, and data engineering tasks because of its user-friendly and powerful capabilities. It simplifies the process of data exploration, cleaning, transformation, and analysis, making it a valuable tool for professionals working with structured data (McKinney, 2017)

NumPy, which stands for "Numerical Python," is a fundamental open-source Python library for numerical and mathematical computations. It is a core building block of the Python scientific computing ecosystem and provides support for large, multi-dimensional arrays and matrices, as well as a wide range of mathematical functions to operate on these arrays. Here are the key functionalities and features of the NumPy package:

1. **Multi-dimensional Arrays:** NumPy introduces the "ndarray", a multi-dimensional array object that can hold data of the same data type. These arrays can have any number of dimensions, allowing you to represent vectors, matrices, and higher-dimensional data structures efficiently.
2. **Mathematical Functions:** NumPy offers a comprehensive set of mathematical functions for operations on arrays. This includes basic arithmetic, trigonometric functions, exponential and logarithmic functions, statistical functions, and more.
3. **Random Number Generation:** NumPy includes a robust random number generator that can produce random data for simulations, experiments, and data augmentation in machine learning.
4. **Linear Algebra Operations:** NumPy supports linear algebra operations, such as matrix multiplication, eigenvalue decomposition, and singular value decomposition, which are essential in various scientific and engineering applications.
5. **Integration with Data Analysis and Visualization:** NumPy is often used in conjunction with other libraries like Pandas for data analysis and Matplotlib or other visualization libraries for data visualization.

NumPy is a fundamental tool for data scientists, engineers, and researchers working in fields like data analysis, machine learning, scientific computing, and more. It forms the foundation for many other Python libraries in the scientific and data analysis ecosystem and is crucial for performing a wide range of numerical and mathematical computations efficiently (McKinney, 2017).

For the multi-criteria decision-making algorithms, pyDecision package was used https://github.com/mcdm-book/pyDecisions . pyDecision is a python library with the following MCDA methods: AHP (Analytic Hierarchy Process); Fuzzy AHP; ARAS (Additive Ratio ASsessment); Fuzzy ARAS; Borda; BWM (Best-Worst Method); CILOS (Criterion Impact LOSs); CoCoSo (COmbined COmpromise SOlution); CODAS (Combinative Distance-based Assessment); Copeland; COPRAS (Complex PRoportional Assessment); Fuzzy COPRAS; CRADIS (Compromise Ranking of Alternatives from Distance to Ideal Solution); CRITIC (CRiteria Importance Through Intercriteria Correlation); DEMATEL (Decision-making Trial and Evaluation Laboratory); Fuzzy DEMATEL; EDAS (Evaluation based on Distance from Average Solution); Fuzzy EDAS; Entropy; ELECTRE (I, I_s, I_v, II, III, IV, Tri-B); GRA (Grey Relational Analysis); IDOCRIW (Integrated Determination of Objective CRIteria Weights); MABAC (Multi-Attributive Border Approximation area Comparison); MACBETH (Measuring Attractiveness by a Categorical Based Evaluation TecHnique); MAIRCA (Multi-Attributive Ideal-Real Comparative Analysis); MARCOS (Measurement of Alternatives and Ranking according to COmpromise Solution); MAUT (Multi-attribute Utility Theory); MEREC (MEthod based on the Removal Effects of Criteria); MOORA (Multi-Objective Optimization on the basis of Ratio Analysis); Fuzzy MOORA; MOOSRA (Multi-Objective Optimization on the Basis of Simple Ratio Analysis); MULTIMOORA (Multi-Objective Optimization on the basis of Ratio Analisys Multiplicative Form); OCRA (Operational Competitiveness RAting); Fuzzy OCRA; ORESTE (Organisation Rangement Et SynThesE de donnees relationnelles); PIV (Proximity Indexed Value); PROMETHEE (I, II, III, IV, V, VI, Gaia); EC PROMETHEE; Regime; ROV (Range Of Value); SAW (Simple Additive Weighting); SMART (Simple Multi-Attribute Rating Technique); SPOTIS (Stable Preference Ordering Towards Ideal Solution); TODIM (TOmada de Decisao Interativa e Multicriterio - Interactive and Multicriteria Decision-making); PSI (Preference Selection Index); TOPSIS (Technique for Order of Preference by Similarity to Ideal Solution); Fuzzy TOPSIS; VIKOR (VIseKriterijumska Optimizacija I Kompromisno

Resenje); Fuzzy VIKOR; WINGS (Weighted Influence Non-linear Gauge System); WSM (Weighted Sum Model); Fuzzy WSM; WPM (Weighted Product Model); Fuzzy WPM; WASPAS (Weighted Aggregates Sum Product Assessment); Fuzzy WASPAS.

Moreover, for modified methods, classes, and functions of pyDecision package were adjusted and published in this GitHub repository https:// github.com/mcdm-book/pyDecisions GitHub is a platform widely used for version control, collaboration, and code sharing in software development. It tracks code changes, facilitates teamwork, supports open-source projects, manages tasks, enables code review, automates testing and deployment, creates project documentation, controls access, builds communities, showcases coding skills, and serves educational purposes. The authors plan to create a pull request to the official GitHub repository of the package to make these changes available for all other researchers through the official pyDecision package.

All the solutions are presented to users with Google Colab notebooks. Links can be found in the Github Repository https://github.com/mcdm-book/pyDecisions, as it is shown in the screen shot below.

Applications for Adressing The Weaknesses of Multi-Criteria Decision-Making Methods Using Python

This repository contains adjusted versions of Python functions of PyDecisions library for book titled Adressing The Weaknesses of Multi-Criteria Decision-Making Methods Using Python. If you would like to reproduce the results presented in Chapter 4.3, please open Colab notebooks mentioned below.

Usage in Google Colab:

- Chapter 4.3.1 ELECTRE III and Modified ELECTRE III (Colab Demo)
- Chapter 4.3.2 PROMETHEE II and Modified PROMETHEE II (Colab Demo)
- Chapter 4.3.3 TOPSIS and Modified TOPSIS (Colab Demo)
- Chapter 4.3.4 VIKOR and Modified VIKOR (Colab Demo)

Figure 4.3: Google Colab notebook links on GitHub repository.

Google Colab is a cloud-based platform for creating and running Jupyter notebooks. It's widely used for coding, data analysis, and machine learning, with built-in Python libraries and GPU support. Users can collaborate, share, and access their work via Google Drive. It's popular in education, research, and development. To start with running code examples, please go to the GitHub repository. You will get to the page shown on Figure 4.3 and you will see the links. Please click the links shown in Figure 4.3. and open Google Colab. Make sure that you are logged in with your Google account. Then to be able to start running the code blocks, click connect shown in Figure 4.4.

Figure 4.4: Google Colab notebook.

Once you are connected to remote machine, you will see "Ram" and "Disk" utilization information on the right top of the screen as shown in Figure 4.5. Worth mentioning that Google Colab version used for this book is free of charge and it doesn't require any subscription. You will also get all data files used for the exercises through the notebook. Everything is ready and put together to Google Colab notebooks so that you can immediately start running Python codes on your own.

Figure 4.5: Google Colab connected.

4.3.1. ELECTRE: *Normalization vs. Standardization*

While normalization will be used for the traditional ELECTRE method, standardization will be used instead of normalization for the modified ELECTRE method.

Traditional ELECTRE III: Normalization

$$r_{ij} = \frac{x_{ij}}{\sqrt{\sum_{k=1}^{n} x_{ij}^2}} \qquad (4.9)$$

Modified ELECTRE III: Standardization

$$x_{ij}^{'} = \frac{x_{ij} - \mu_x}{\sigma_x} \text{ formula will be used.} \qquad (4.10)$$

4.3.1.1. *Application for Traditional ELECTRE vs. Modified ELECTRE*

In this subsection, the comparison of the above-mentioned modified ELECTRE III and traditional ELECTRE III methods for the IHDI dataset will be discussed.

4.3.1.1.1. Normalization vs. Standardization

Conversion of the decision matrix elements (indicators) to the same unit in MCDM methods will be shown on ELECTRE III. For this purpose, to identify the world development levels, first the traditional ELECTRE III method which uses the normalization method to convert the decision matrix elements to the same unit, will be applied to the data from IHDI, which later will be followed by the application of the modified ELECTRE III method, which uses the standardization method. Thus, the effects of normalization and standardization on the ELECTRE III method will be examined.

For the following applications you can find the Python code here. This link will re-direct you to Google Colab notebook. Within this notebook you will be able to run the Python codes to reproduce the results below without installing any component to your computer.

4.3.1.1.2. *Traditional ELECTRE III: Normalization*

Step 0: Defining P, Q, V and w:

```
P = [0, 0, 0, 0, 0]
Q = [0.04, 0.1, 0.1, 0.1, 0.1]
V = [0.1, 0.2, 0.2, 0.2, 0.2]
W = [0.2, 0.2, 0.2, 0.2, 0.2]
```

Step 1: Creating the decision matrix:

```
np.array([
[0.959, 0.915, 0.94543341, 0.93780236, 0.86439586],
[0.961, 0.908, 0.94810366, 0.91168243, 0.86583901],
[0.948, 0.898, 0.91584883, 0.90868089, 0.86999746],
[0.962, 0.894, 0.95386773, 0.90178962, 0.8296717],
[0.94, 0.89, 0.92795415, 0.90667729, 0.83884948],
[0.945, 0.886, 0.92685716, 0.85597718, 0.8773704],
[0.947, 0.885, 0.94368242, 0.88472682, 0.8301875],
.
.
.
.])
```

Step 2: Creating the normalized decision matrix:

```
array    ([0.10441004,    0.11677943,    0.10580386,
0.12159295,  0.11952489],  [0.10462778,  0.11588603,
0.10610269,  0.11820631,  0.11972444],  [0.10321242,
0.11460975,  0.10249304,  0.11781714,  0.12029946],
[0.10473666,  0.11409924,  0.10674775,  0.11692363,
0.11472339],  [0.10234143,  0.11358873,  0.10384775,
0.11755735,  0.11599245],  [0.1028858,  0.11307822,
0.10372499, 0.11098371, 0.12131895]
.
.
.
.])
```

Step 2: Call Electre III Function

```
>global_concordance, credibility, rank_D, rank_A,
rank_N, rank_P = electre_iii(mcdm_data_normalized,
          P = P,
          Q = Q,
          V = V,
          W = W,
          graph = False)
```

Step 3: Check global concordance matrix:

```
>global_concordance
array([[0., 0.4, 0.8, ..., 1., 1., 1.],
  [0.6, 0., 0.8, ..., 1., 1., 1.],
  [0.2, 0.2, 0., ..., 1., 1., 1.],
  ...,
  [0., 0., 0., ..., 0., 0.6, 0.4],
  [0., 0., 0., ..., 0.4, 0., 0.6],
  [0., 0., 0., ..., 0.6, 0.4, 0.]])
```

Step 4: Check credibility matrix:

```
>np.ndarray.round(credibility, decimals = 2)
array([[0., 0.4,0.8, ..., 1., 1.,1.],
  [0.6, 0., 0.8, ..., 1., 1., 1.],
  [0.2, 0.2,0., ..., 1., 1., 1.],
  ...,
  [0., 0., 0., ..., 0., 0.6, 0.4],
  [0., 0., 0., ..., 0.39, 0., 0.6],
  [0., 0., 0., ..., 0.6, 0.4, 0.]])
```

Step 5: Ranking descending (first 10):

1. Iceland
2. Norway
3. Switzerland
4. Finland
5. Sweden

6. Australia
7. Denmark
8. Germany; Netherlands
9. Ireland
10. Slovenia; New Zealand; Canada

4.3.1.1.3. Modified ELECTRE III: Standardization

Step 0: Defining P, Q, V and w:

```
P = [0, 0, 0, 0, 0]
Q = [0.04, 0.1, 0.1, 0.1, 0.1]
V = [0.1, 0.2, 0.2, 0.2, 0.2]
W = [0.2, 0.2, 0.2, 0.2, 0.2]
```

Step 1: Creating the decision matrix:

```
np.array([
[0.959, 0.915, 0.94543341, 0.93780236, 0.86439586],
[0.961, 0.908, 0.94810366, 0.91168243, 0.86583901],
[0.948, 0.898, 0.91584883, 0.90868089, 0.86999746],
[0.962, 0.894, 0.95386773, 0.90178962, 0.8296717],
[0.94, 0.89, 0.92795415, 0.90667729, 0.83884948],
[0.945, 0.886, 0.92685716, 0.85597718, 0.8773704],
[0.947, 0.885, 0.94368242, 0.88472682, 0.8301875],
.
.
.
.])
```

Step 2: Creating the standardized decision matrix:

```
array([[1.54099726e+00,1.68004408e+00,1.43745081e+
00, 1.59160776e+00, 1.78545781e+00],
[1.55382040e+00,1.64290552e+00,1.45269593e+
00,1.47748461e+00, 1.79370431e+00],
[1.47046994e+00,1.58985042e+00,1.26854497e+
00,1.46437026e+00, 1.81746673e+00],
.
```

```
.
.
.])
```

Step 2: Call Electre III Function

```
>global_concordance, credibility, rank_D, rank_A,
rank_N, rank_P = electre_iii(mcdm_data_standardized,
    P = P,
    Q = Q,
    V = V,
    W = W,
    graph = False)
```

Step 3: Check global concordance matrix:

```
>global_concordance

array([[0., 0.4, 0.8, ..., 1., 1., 1.],
[0.6, 0., 0.8, ..., 1., 1., 1.],
[0.2, 0.2, 0., ..., 1., 1., 1.],
...,
[0., 0., 0., ..., 0., 0.6, 0.4],
[0., 0., 0., ..., 0.4, 0., 0.6],
[0., 0., 0., ..., 0.6, 0.4, 0.]])
```

Step 4: Check credibility matrix:

```
>np.ndarray.round(credibility, decimals = 2)
array([[0., 0.4, 0.8, ..., 1., 1., 1.],
[0.6, 0., 0.8, ..., 1., 1., 1.],
[0.0045, 0.0038, 0., ..., 1., 1., 1.],
...,
[0., 0., 0., ..., 0., 0.1071, 0.],
[0., 0., 0., ..., 0., 0., 0.],
[0., 0., 0., ..., 0., 0.0089, 0.]
])
```

Step 5: Ranking descending (Top 10):

1. Iceland
2. Norway
3. Switzerland
4. Finland
5. Sweden
6. Australia
7. Denmark
8. Germany
9. Netherlands
10. Ireland

4.3.1.1.4. Comparison of Results (Top 10)

As a result of the ranking results given in Table 4.8 it is seen that there are partial differences between the traditional ELECTRE and modified ELECTRE results.

Table 4.8: Comparison of Traditional and Modified ELECTRE III Results

Rank	Traditional ELECTRE III	Modified ELECTRE III
1	Iceland	Iceland
2	Norway	Norway
3	Switzerland	Switzerland
4	Finland	Finland
5	Sweden	Sweden
6	Australia	Australia
7	Denmark	Denmark
8	Germany; Netherlands	Germany
9	Ireland	Netherlands
10	Slovenia; New Zealand; Canada	Ireland

4.3.2. PROMETHEE: *Differentiation of Weighting Method*

While equal weighting is preferred as weighting in the traditional PROMETHEE method, Saaty weighting method will be used in the modified PROMETHEE method.

4.3.2.1. Traditional PROMETHEE

Equal weighting will be used. Equal weighting is 1/n, see Section 3.1.2 for details.

4.3.2.2. Modified PROMETHEE

Saaty weighting method will be used. see Section 3.1.2 for details about how the Saaty weighting method is done.

4.3.2.3. Application for Traditional PROMETHEE vs Modified PROMETHEE

4.3.2.3.1. Differentiation of Weighting Method

The differentiation of weighting in MCDM methods will be shown on the PROMETHEE method. For this purpose, in order to identify the world growth levels, by using the data from IHDI, equal weights method will be applied first, which will be followed by the application of different weighting methods, AHP and Best-Worst methods. The final application will be the modified PROMETHEE method. The results from each weighting method will be compared, thus, the effects of different weighting criteria on the PROMETHEE method will be examined. For the following applications you can find the Python code here. This link will re-direct you to Google Colab notebook. Within this notebook you will be able to run the Python codes to reproduce the results below without installing any component to your computer.

4.3.2.3.2. Traditional PROMETHEE

Step 1: Determination of F

We decided to go with type 5 for this example.

```
F = ['t5', 't5', 't5', 't5','t5']
```

Step 2: Determination of weights

```
W = [0.2, 0.2, 0.2, 0.2, 0.2]
```

Step 3: Determination of Q, P, S

```
Q = [0.3, 0.3, 0.3, 0.3, 0.3]
S = [0.4, 0.4, 0.4, 0.4, 0.4]
P = [0.5, 0.5, 0.5, 0.5, 0.5]
```

Step 4: Calculation of preference matrix

```
preference_matrix
[[0. 0. 0. … 1. 1. 1.]
 [0. 0. 0. … 1. 1. 1.]
 [0. 0. 0. … 1. 1. 1.]
 ...
 [0. 0. 0. … 0. 0. 0.]
 [0. 0. 0. … 0. 0. 0.]
 [0. 0. 0. … 0. 0. 0.]]
```

Step 5: Calculation of the positive and negative outranking flows

```
positive_flow
[3.16294560e-01    3.10414488e-01    2.96681209e-
01   2.92525578e-01   2.83103205e-01   2.88041978e-
01   2.80147063e-01   2.74623420e-01   2.72496241e-01
2.63027968e-01    2.67562312e-01    2.69707620e-01
2.50701252e-01    2.46277168e-01    2.37246733e-01
2.45156000e-01    2.32216483e-01    2.37605947e-01
2.27038153e-01 2.34330978e-01
.
.
.
]
negative_flow
[0.00000000e+00    0.00000000e+00    0.00000000e+
00   0.00000000e+00   0.00000000e+00   0.00000000e+
00   0.00000000e+00   0.00000000e+00   0.00000000e+00
0.00000000e+00 0.00000000e+00 0.00000000e+00
.
.
```

```
2.65355718e-01      3.05351561e-01      2.97364679e-01
3.04363683e-01      3.23232673e-01      3.24940287e-01
3.11692654e-01      3.39052801e-01      3.31024769e-01
4.20634845e-01 4.30869277e-01 4.29610528e-01]
```

Step 6. Calculation of net outranking flow (the PROMETHEE II complete ranking)

1. Iceland
2. Norway
3. Denmark
4. Switzerland
5. Ireland
6. Finland
7. Sweden
8. Germany
9. Netherlands
10. Belgium

4.3.2.3.3. Modified PROMETHEE

Step 1: Determination of F

We decided to go with type 5 for this example.

```
F = ["t5", "t5", "t5", "t5", "t5"]
```

Step 2: Determination of weights

Weights were defined by using AHP

```
# AHP

# Parameters
weight_derivation =                        "geometric"

# Dataset
dataset = np.array([
#HDI ia-HDI ia-LE ia-EI ia-II
[1, 1/3, 1/5, 1, 1/4], #HDI
[3, 1, 1/2, 2, 1/3], #ia-HDI
```

```
[5, 2, 1, 4, 5], #ia-LE
[1, 1/2, 1/4, 1, 1/4], #ia-EI
[4, 3, 1/5, 4, 1] #ia-II
])
```

```
w(g1): 0.069
w(g2): 0.156
w(g3): 0.451
w(g4): 0.078
w(g5): 0.246
```

Step 3: Determination of Q,P,S

```
Q = [0.3, 0.3, 0.3, 0.3, 0.3]
S = [0.4, 0.4, 0.4, 0.4, 0.4]
P = [0.5, 0.5, 0.5, 0.5, 0.5]
```

Step 4: Calculation of preference matrix

```
array([
[0., 0., 0., ..., 1., 1., 1.],
[0., 0., 0., ..., 1., 1.,1.],
[0., 0., 0., ..., 1., 1., 1.],...,
[0., 0., 0., ..., 0., 0., 0.],
[0., 0., 0., ..., 0., 0., 0.],
[0., 0., 0., ..., 0., 0., 0.]])
```

Step 5: Calculation of the positive and negative outranking flows

```
positive_flow
array([
2.98958999e-01,  2.97524573e-01,  2.77343399e-01,
2.80284307e-01,  2.67302040e-01,  2.80463247e-01,
2.70124601e-01,  2.47930146e-01,  2.57882228e-01,
2.45524238e-01,  2.58458111e-01,  2.58576510e-01,
2.27896906e-01,  2.27874186e-01,  2.30432144e-01,
2.45888925e-01,  2.04926622e-01,  2.43487703e-01,
2.03042496e-01,  2.35532353e-01,  2.31713876e-01,
1.71218853e-01, 2.31386482e-01, 2.18058237e-01,....
```

```
])

negative_flow
array([0.00000000e+00, 0.00000000e+00, 0.00000000e+
00, 0.00000000e+00, 0.00000000e+00, 0.00000000e+00,
0.00000000e+00, 0.00000000e+00, 0.00000000e+00,
0.00000000e+00, 0.00000000e+00, 0.00000000e+
00, 0.00000000e+00, 0.00000000e+00, 0.00000000e+00,
0.00000000e+00, 0.00000000e+00, 0.00000000e+
00, 0.00000000e+00, 0.00000000e+00, 0.00000000e+00,
0.00000000e+00, 0.00000000e+00, 0.00000000e+00, . . .
.
.
.
])
```

Step 6. Calculation of net outranking flow (the PROMETHEE II complete ranking)

1. Iceland
2. Norway
3. Ireland
4. Switzerland
5. Denmark
6. Sweden
7. Finland
8. Belgium
9. Australia
10. Netherlands

4.3.2.4. Comparison of Results

As a result of the ranking results given in Table 4.9, it is seen that there are differences between the traditional PROMETHEE and modified PROMETHEE results.

Table 4.9: Comparison of Traditional and Modified PROMETHEE Results

Rank	Traditional PROMETHEE	Modified PROMETHEE
1	Iceland	Iceland
2	Norway	Norway
3	Denmark	Ireland
4	Switzerland	Switzerland
5	Ireland	Denmark
6	Finland	Sweden
7	Sweden	Finland
8	Germany	Belgium
9	Netherlands	Australia
10	Belgium	Netherlands

4.3.3. TOPSIS: *Differentiation of Measurement Method*

While using Euclidean distance in the traditional TOPSIS method, in the modified TOPSIS method, one of the non-Euclidean city block, Minkowski, or Chebyshev distances in the Minkowski Family can be preferred instead of normalization.

4.3.3.1. Traditional TOPSIS

Euclidean distance is used.

$$D_i^+ = \sqrt{\sum_{j=1}^{n}\left(y_{ij} + y_j^+\right)^2} \tag{4.11}$$

$$D_i^- = \sqrt{\sum_{j=1}^{n}\left(y_{ij} - y_j^-\right)^2} \tag{4.12}$$

4.3.3.2. Modified TOPSIS

4.3.3.2.1. L_p Minkowski Family

The distance formulas of the L_p Minkowski Family are given in Equations 4.14.16 (Anandan & Uthra, 2017)
Euclidean L_1:

$$d_i = \sqrt{\sum_{j=1}^{n} \left| a_{ij} - b_{ij} \right|^2} \qquad (4.13)$$

City block L_1 :

$$d_i = \sum_{j=1}^{n} \left| a_{ij} - b_{ij} \right| \qquad (4.14)$$

Minkowski L_p :

$$d_i = \sqrt[p]{\sum_{j=1}^{n} \left| a_{ij} - b_{ij} \right|^p} \qquad (4.15)$$

Chebyshev L_∞ :

$$d_i = \left| a_{ij} - b_{ij} \right| \qquad (4.16)$$

4.3.3.3. Application for Traditional TOPSIS vs. Modified TOPSIS

4.3.3.3.1. Differentiation of Measurement Method

The differentiation of measurement methods in MCDM methods will be shown on the TOPSIS method. For this purpose, by using data from IHDI, the traditional TOPSIS method will be applied first to identify the world development levels, which later will be followed by the application of the modified TOPSIS method where the measurement has been changed. The results from each method will be compared, thus, the effects of different sorting criteria on the TOPSIS method will be examined. All the results are reproducible. For the following applications you can find the Python code here. This link will re-direct you to Google Colab notebook. Within this notebook you will be able to run the Python codes to reproduce the results below without installing any component to your computer.

4.3.3.3.2. Traditional TOPSIS: Euclidean Distance

Step 1: Creating the decision matrix:

```
np.array([
[0.959, 0.915, 0.94543341, 0.93780236, 0.86439586],
[0.961, 0.908, 0.94810366, 0.91168243, 0.86583901],
[0.948, 0.898, 0.91584883, 0.90868089, 0.86999746],
[0.962, 0.894, 0.95386773, 0.90178962, 0.8296717],
[0.94, 0.89, 0.92795415, 0.90667729, 0.83884948],
[0.945, 0.886, 0.92685716, 0.85597718, 0.8773704],
[0.947, 0.885, 0.94368242, 0.88472682, 0.8301875],
.
.
.
.])
```

Step 2. Determining the weighting vector

```
weights = np.array([[0.2, 0.2, 0.2, 0.2, 0.2]])
```

Step 3. Determining the criterion type

```
criterion_type = ['max', 'max', 'max', 'max', 'max']
```

Step 4. Normalized the decision matrix.

```
array([[0.10441004,    0.11677943,    0.10580386,
0.12159295, 0.11952489], [0.10462778, 0.11588603,
0.10610269, 0.11820631, 0.11972444], [0.10321242,
0.11460975, 0.10249304, 0.11781714, 0.12029946],
[0.10473666, 0.11409924, 0.10674775, 0.11692363,
0.11472339], [0.10234143, 0.11358873, 0.10384775,
0.11755735, 0.11599245], [0.1028858, 0.11307822,
0.10372499, 0.11098371, 0.12131895], [0.10310355,
0.11295059, 0.10560791, 0.11471131, 0.11479471],
[0.10255918, 0.11269534, 0.10082911, 0.11891004,
0.11521984],
.
.
.
]])
```

Step 5. Calculating PIS

```
array([0.00084409, 0.0010416, 0.00170854, 0.00179644,
0.00193679, 0.0025637, 0.00222051, 0.002391, 0.002581,
0.00268382,   0.00318926,   0.00285157,   0.00362087,
0.00373088,   0.00411752,   0.00446627,   0.00429671,
0.00465689,   0.00424314,   0.0044705,    0.00512905,
0.0052742,    0.00595135,   0.00583397,   0.00570904,
0.00603518,   0.00618368,   0.00592192,   0.00632072,
0.00673472,   0.00683517,   0.00700243,   0.00733797,
0.00727625,   0.00778319,
.
.
.
]])
```

Step 6. Calculating NIS

```
array([0.03783913, 0.03745813, 0.03699359, 0.03671674,
0.03647647,   0.03633408,   0.03618681,   0.03625034,
0.03586465,   0.0357567,    0.03574003,   0.03566913,
0.03526425,   0.03495719,   0.03429802,   0.0343742,
0.0345061,    0.03420485,   0.03430931,   0.03412585,
0.03363219,   0.03330606,   0.03340075,   0.03294315,
0.03315848,   0.03258953,   0.03276255,   0.03254878,
0.03262053,   0.03184363,   0.03202357,   0.03133798,
0.03157458,   0.03119572,   0.03119603,   0.03114665,
0.0311373,    0.03017436,   0.02968084,   0.02911069,
.
.
.
]])
```

Step 7. Calculating the overall performance index

```
array([0.9781795, 0.97294536, 0.95585398, 0.95335519,
0.94958017,   0.93409136,   0.94218526,   0.93812317,
0.93286634,   0.93018253,   0.91807545,   0.92597297,
0.90688295,   0.90356498,   0.89281632,   0.88500981,
0.88926799,   0.88016766,   0.88993862,   0.88417298,
0.86767576,   0.86329274,   0.84876669,   0.84955127,
```

```
0.8531155,    0.8437482,    0.84122516,    0.84606668,
0.83768575, 0.82542755,
.
.
.
]])
```

Step 8. Ranking (top 10)

1. Iceland
2. Norway
3. Denmark
4. Switzerland
5. Finland
6. Sweden
7. Germany
8. Ireland
9. Netherlands
10. Slovenia

4.3.3.3.3. Modified TOPSIS: Chebyshev Distance

Step 1: Creating the decision matrix:

```
np.array([
[0.959, 0.915, 0.94543341, 0.93780236, 0.86439586],
[0.961, 0.908, 0.94810366, 0.91168243, 0.86583901],
[0.948, 0.898, 0.91584883, 0.90868089, 0.86999746],
[0.962, 0.894, 0.95386773, 0.90178962, 0.8296717],
[0.94, 0.89, 0.92795415, 0.90667729, 0.83884948],
[0.945, 0.886, 0.92685716, 0.85597718, 0.8773704],
[0.947, 0.885, 0.94368242, 0.88472682, 0.8301875],
.
.
.
.])
```

Step 2. Determining the weighting vector

```
weights = np.array([[0.2, 0.2, 0.2, 0.2, 0.2]])
```

Step 3. Determining the criterion type

```
criterion_type = ['max', 'max', 'max', 'max', 'max']
```

Step 4. Normalized the decision matrix

```
array([[0.10441004,    0.11677943,    0.10580386,
0.12159295,  0.11952489], [0.10462778,  0.11588603,
0.10610269,  0.11820631,  0.11972444], [0.10321242,
0.11460975,  0.10249304,  0.11781714,  0.12029946],
[0.10473666,  0.11409924,  0.10674775,  0.11692363,
0.11472339], [0.10234143,  0.11358873,  0.10384775,
0.11755735,  0.11599245], [0.1028858,  0.11307822,
0.10372499,  0.11098371,  0.12131895], [0.10310355,
0.11295059,  0.10560791,  0.11471131,  0.11479471],
[0.10255918,  0.11269534,  0.10082911,  0.11891004,
0.11521984],
.
.
]])
```

Step 5. Calculating PIS with Chebyshev distance

```
[array([0.00076123,    0.00070146,    0.00142339,
0.00131911,  0.00115245,  0.00212185,  0.00137633,
0.00175618,  0.0016378,  0.00159834,  0.00280175,
0.00204589,  0.00301459,  0.00296441,  0.00275139,
0.00371714,  0.0033116,  0.00321271,  0.00266256,
0.00281294,  0.00360899,  0.00316408,  0.0042397,
0.00454773,  0.00350132,  0.00439075,  0.00433083,
0.00324485,  0.00490485,  0.00390158,  0.0042226,
0.00380408,  0.00428631,  0.00388754,  0.00545519,
0.00451854,  0.00571851,  0.00655533,  0.00448887,
0.00573356,
.
.
]])
```

Step 6. Calculating NIS with Chebyshev distance

```
array([0.02019583, 0.0195185, 0.01944066, 0.01926196,
0.01938871,   0.01945012,   0.0188195,   0.01965924,
0.01855802,   0.0191718,    0.01911125,  0.01864051,
0.01958765,   0.01904679,   0.01751917,  0.01823627,
0.01924866,   0.01737929,   0.0183982,   0.01738289,
0.01658683,   0.01859214,   0.01666532,  0.01722958,
0.01878565,   0.01678515,   0.01593863,  0.01777902,
0.01752542,   0.01711385,
.
.
]])
```

Step 7. Calculating the overall performance index

```
array([0.96367672,    0.96530838,    0.93177771,
0.93590647,   0.9438955,    0.9016387,    0.93185091,
0.91799466,   0.91890388,   0.9230464,    0.87214209,
0.90109984,   0.86662419,   0.86532244,   0.86426686,
0.83068064,   0.85321111,   0.84398256,   0.87357708,
0.86071693,   0.82130005,   0.85456671,   0.79719227,
0.79117104,   0.8428983,
.
.
]])
```

Step 8. Ranking (Top 10)

1. Norway
2. Iceland
3. Finland
4. Switzerland
5. Sweden
6. Denmark
7. Slovenia
8. Netherlands
9. Germany
10. Ireland

4.3.3.3.4. Comparison of Results (Top 10)

As a result of the ranking results given in Table 4.10, it is seen that there are differences between the traditional TOPSIS and modified TOPSIS results.

Table 4.10: Comparison of Traditional and Modified TOPSIS Results

Rank	Traditional TOPSIS	Modified TOPSIS
1	Iceland	Norway
2	Norway	Iceland
3	Denmark	Finland
4	Switzerland	Switzerland
5	Finland	Sweden
6	Sweden	Denmark
7	Germany	Slovenia
8	Ireland	Netherlands
9	Netherlands	Germany
10	Slovenia	Ireland

4.3.4. VIKOR: *Differentiation of Sorting Criteria*

In the traditional VIKOR method, the " v " value in the formula is usually considered as " 0.5 " while calculating the value of Q_i whereas in the modified VIKOR method, different values will be taken for the " v^* " value.

4.3.4.1. Traditional VIKOR

$$Q_i = v.\left(\frac{S_i - S^*}{S^- - S^*}\right) + (1 - v)\left(\frac{R_i - R^*}{R^- - R^*}\right) \qquad (4.17)$$

For the Q_i used in the Traditional VIKOR method, the v value in the above formula is generally considered as " 0.5 ", calculations are performed and sorted according to the largest Q.

4.3.4.2. Modified VIKOR

$$Q_i = v^*\left(\frac{S_i - S^*}{S^- - S^*}\right) + (1 - v^*)\left(\frac{R_i - R^*}{R^- - R^*}\right) \qquad (4.18)$$

Different values will be used for v^* in the formula (for application assumed v* is 0.6).

4.3.4.3. Application for Traditional VIKOR vs. Modified VIKOR

4.3.4.3.1. Differentiation of Sorting Criteria

The differentiation of sorting criteria in MCDM methods will be shown on the VIKOR method. For this purpose, by using data from IHDI, the traditional VIKOR method will be applied first to identify the world development levels, which later will be followed by applying the modified VIKOR method where the sorting criteria has been changed. The results from each method will be compared, thus, the effects of different sorting criteria on the VIKOR method will be examined. For the following applications you can find the Python code here. This link will re-direct you to Google Colab notebook. Within this notebook you will be able to run the Python codes to reproduce the results below without installing any component to your computer.

4.3.4.3.2. Traditional VIKOR (v=0.5)

Step 1: Define weights.

```
weights = np.array([[0.2, 0.2, 0.2, 0.2, 0.2]])
```

Step 2: Define criterion types.

```
criterion_type = ['min', 'min', 'min', 'min', 'min']
```

Step 3: Determine the best x_j^* and the worst x_i^- values of all criterion functions

```
best
[0.385 0.24 0.30360281 0.15898694 0.17406066]
worst
[0.962 0.915 0.97944405 0.93780236 0.8773704]
```

Step 4: Compute the values of S_i and R_i

```
si
[0.98520589 0.97831804 0.96171566 0.9633969 0.95078256
 0.94894023 0.94828175 0.94250969 0.937158 0.92875612
 0.94096538 0.93238212 0.92211934 0.91652974 0.89937042
```

```
0.90460798 0.90174741 0.90468379 0.88648894 0.89963688
0.89077289 0.86384904 0.8921977 0.86885014 0.86245462
0.85922412 0.87339355 0.84350662 0.86310607 0.81938358
.
.
.
]
ri
[0.2  0.19965338  0.19790336  0.2  0.19259259  0.2
   0.19480069
0.1946862 0.19272097 0.18985903 0.19618718 0.19167499
0.19397718 0.19098787 0.18405546 0.18890815 0.19062023
0.19769561    0.18405686    0.19114316    0.1919546
   0.18411862 0.2
0.18383695 0.18603497 0.18143038 0.19202773 0.17606632
0.18509532 0.17418965
.
.
.
]
```

Step 5: Compute the value Q_i

```
qi
[1.   0.99545214   0.9820487   0.98852992   0.96212146
   0.98092667
0.96670075 0.9633594 0.95529856 0.94323973 0.96655405
0.9499945 0.95074268 0.93982293 0.91229212 0.92800103
0.93106699 0.95149915 0.90552105 0.93135296 0.92885724
0.89377885 0.95108388 0.89565716
.
.
]
```

Step 6: Rank the alternatives (Top 10)

1.   Norway
2.   Iceland
3.   Denmark

4. Slovenia
5. Ireland
6. Austria
7. Switzerland
8. Netherlands
9. Finland
10. Australia

4.3.4.3.3. Modified VIKOR ($v^* = 0.6$ assumed)

Step 1: Define weights.

```
weights = np.array([[0.2, 0.2, 0.2, 0.2, 0.2]])
```

Step 2: Define criterion types.

```
criterion_type = ['min', 'min', 'min', 'min', 'min']
```

Step 3: Determine the best x_j^* and the worst x_i^- values of all criterion functions.

```
best
[0.385 0.24 0.30360281 0.15898694 0.17406066]
worst
[0.962 0.915 0.97944405 0.93780236 0.8773704]
```

Step 4: Compute the values of S_i and R_i

```
si
[0.98520589 0.97831804 0.96171566 0.9633969 0.95078256
0.94894023 0.94828175 0.94250969 0.937158 0.92875612
0.94096538 0.93238212 0.92211934 0.91652974 0.89937042
0.90460798 0.90174741 0.90468379 0.88648894 0.89963688
0.89077289 0.86384904 0.8921977 0.86885014
.
.
.
]
ri
```

```
[0.2   0.19965338   0.19790336   0.2   0.19259259   0.2
0.194800690.1946862 0.19272097 0.18985903 0.19618718
0.191674990.19397718 0.19098787 0.18405546 0.18890815
0.190620230.19769561 0.18405686 0.19114316 0.1919546
0.184118620.20.18383695       0.18603497       0.18143038
0.19202773 0.176066320.18509532 0.17418965
.
.
.
]
```

Step 5: Compute the value Q_i

```
qi
[1.   0.99491269   0.98069724   0.9862359   0.96245541
   0.97711201
0.96559274 0.96170537 0.95413085 0.94271625 0.96393622
0.94888288 0.94732241 0.93741071 0.9117762 0.92544517
0.92729615 0.94425961 0.90364942 0.92708092 0.9232196
0.88949283 0.94130065 0.89204758 0.89270535 0.88083291
0.91240733 0.85945776 0.89110978 0.84022538
.
.
.
]
```

Step 6: Rank the alternatives (Top 10)

1.   Norway
2.   Iceland
3.   Denmark
4.   Slovenia
5.   Finland
6.   New Zealand
7.   Switzerland
8.   Sweden
9.   Ireland
10.   Australia

4.3.4.3.4. Comparison of Results (Top 10)

As a result of the ranking results given in Table 4.11, it is seen that there are differences between the traditional VIKOR and modified VIKOR results.

Table 4.11: Comparison of Traditional and Modified VIKOR Results

Rank	Traditional VIKOR	Modified VIKOR
1	Norway	Norway
2	Iceland	Iceland
3	Denmark	Denmark
4	Slovenia	Slovenia
5	Ireland	Finland
6	Austria	New Zealand
7	Switzerland	Switzerland
8	Netherlands	Sweden
9	Finland	Ireland
10	Australia	Australia

Table 4.12: Comparison of Traditional and Modified Results of ELECTRE, TOPSIS, PROMETHEE and VIKOR Methods

Rank	1	2	3	4	5	6	7	8	9	10
Traditional ELECTRE	Iceland	Norway	Switzerland	Finland	Sweden	Australia	Denmark	Germany; Netherlands	Ireland	Slovenia; New Zealand; Canada
Modified ELECTRE	Iceland	Norway	Switzerland	Finland	Sweden	Australia	Denmark	Germany	Netherlands	Ireland
Traditional PROMETHEE	Iceland	Norway	Denmark	Switzerland	Ireland	Finland	Sweden	Germany	Netherlands	Belgium
Modified PROMETHEE	Iceland	Norway	Ireland	Switzerland	Denmark	Sweden	Finland	Belgium	Australia	Netherlands
Traditional TOPSIS	Iceland	Norway	Denmark	Switzerland	Finland	Sweden	Germany	Ireland	Netherlands	Slovenia
Modified TOPSIS	Norway	Iceland	Finland	Switzerland	Sweden	Denmark	Slovenia	Netherlands	Germany	Ireland
Traditional VIKOR	Norway	Iceland	Denmark	Slovenia	Ireland	Austria	Switzerland	Netherlands	Finland	Australia
Modified VIKOR	Norway	Iceland	Denmark	Slovenia	Finland	New Zealand	Switzerland	Sweden	Ireland	Australia
HDI	Switzerland	Norway	Iceland	Hong Kong, China (SAR)	Australia	Denmark	Sweden	Ireland	Germany	Netherlands
IHDI	Iceland	Norway	Denmark	Switzerland	Ireland	Sweden	Germany	Netherlands	Australia	Hong Kong, China (SAR)

A complete list of rankings for all countries and methods can be found in Appendix I.

Table 4.12 shows that there are differences between the traditional rankings of the ELECTRE, PROMETHEE, TOPSIS and VIKOR methods when ranking countries according to IHDI data. These differences are also present in the modified results of the methods. In addition, the table shows that there are differences between the traditional ranking of each method and its modified ranking. In addition, when the traditional and modified top 10 ranking results of the ELECTRE, PROMETHEE, TOPSIS and VIKOR methods given in Table 18 and covered in the book are examined together, it is seen that all rankings are different from each other. This clearly shows how important the elements that are defined as the weaknesses of MCDM methods in the book are. It is clear that how the methods are handled affects the ranking results and that this can lead to very different results in the solution of decision problems to be considered.

Conclusion and Suggestions

In this study named "Addressing the Weaknesses of Multi-Criteria Decision-Making Methods Using Python", the significance of MCDM methods, which can help us choose the most appropriate option among the available alternatives in the process of realizing the decision-making action at every stage of our lives, has been attempted to be emphasized once more. The study's primary goal was to highlight the significance of MCDM methods while also highlighting how different approaches could lead to different results. The word "weakness" is used in the book to describe this circumstance.

As previously stated, none of the MCDM approaches actually outperforms the others. Basically, the majority of the methods involve the fundamental steps of reducing the decision matrix to a single unit, choosing the appropriate weighting method, figuring out the measurement value, and sorting the outcomes. These stages can be realized using a variety of strategies. The "modified" nature of this situation undoubtedly allows for the derivation of various outcomes.

The "traditional" ELECTRE, PROMEETHE, TOPSIS and VIKOR methods—the most well-known MCDM approaches in the literature—are compared to "modified" approaches in the book. The four previously mentioned main headings are used to organize the discussion of the modification approaches for this purpose:

1. Deciding on a conversion strategy, such as normalization or standardization, to bring the decision matrix to the same unit.
2. Choosing the weighting strategy.
3. Choosing (differentiating) the measurement technique.
4. Deciding on a ranking/sorting/ordering strategy.

With the exception of ELECTRE, PROMEETHE, TOPSIS and VIKOR, it is possible to apply these steps, which are referred to as a "weakness" in the book, in a similar manner for other MCDM methods. The last two weaknesses, however, may vary depending on the content and structure of the MCDM method, whereas the first two weaknesses mentioned above may apply to all MCDM methods.

Traditional MCDM methods can produce different results depending on how different processing techniques are used. Real data were used in the book in order to provide a concrete way to observe this situation. Data from IHDI was used for this. Due to the increasing importance of comparing the levels of development of different nations in our developing world, this data set was chosen for use in applications. By highlighting the "weaknesses" of these methods, it is also highlighted how MCDM methods can be used to create country rankings and how the outcomes can vary.

As stated earlier, IHDI is a distribution-sensitive approach rather than association-sensitive. It combines the average achievements of countries in health, education and income, and how these achievements are distributed among the country's population, by "discounting" the average value of each dimension according to the level of inequality. In this way, two countries can have the same average HDI value, but on the other hand, they can have different success distributions.

Three basic variables used in the calculation of IHDI in applications, Inequality-adjusted life expectancy index, Inequality-adjusted education index and Inequality-adjusted income index dimensions, were taken as variables and their rankings were tried to be determined by calculating IHDI values for the world countries.

All the traditional and modified methods covered in the book are actually an alternative to the world's HDI or IHDI rankings. The methods dealt with in the calculation of the HDI and IHDI values, as detailed in Section 4, are often sufficiently scientific and appropriate by researchers based on geometric or arithmetic averages. Therefore, new approaches to literature have been introduced, stating that different approaches should be used in the calculation of HDI and IHDI values. In particular, MCDM methods have been the preferred approaches in this area. The book literature will undoubtedly be a guide for researchers, as it will make a new contribution in this regard.

Undoubtedly, another important feature of the book is that all these studies listed above are shared as open source in Python programming language and the reader can easily perform all application trials. Readers will be able to rerun all codes via Google Colab without having to install any software on their computers. The authors provide open-source code for all calculations in their GitHub repository. Every calculation performed within the parameters of the book adds to the PyDecision Python library, which is already available. In addition to the book, the authors also significantly advance the field of open-source software. Each code is reusable and open to detailed analysis. The authors also have plans to compile these codes for R users and publish an R package in the future.

The implementation steps of the traditional ELECTRE, PROMEETHE, TOPSIS and VIKOR methods as well as the implementation steps of the modifications of these methods, which express a different solution approach, were used for the study's real data-based applications. Since the MCDM methods were established first, the data preprocessing step was completed to convert the original IHDI data into a format that can be used with them.

First, the conventional ELECTRE method was used, and when the method was modified, the standardization approach was chosen rather than the conventional ELECTRE method's normalization. Thus, the first weakness, which is the step of differentiating the preferred method in bringing the data to the same unit, has been realized.

The second weakness of the preferred weighting method, which is expressed in the following application, is discussed along with the conventional PROMETHEE method to demonstrate the various outcomes that this weakness may produce. The PROMETHEE method was modified and Saaty's weighting method was chosen.

Next, the conventional TOPSIS approach was used. The step of selecting a different measurement method, which is referred to as the third weakness, was carried out in the modification of the TOPSIS method. Using the non-Euclidean Chebyshev distance in the Minkowski Family instead of the Euclidean distance used in the conventional TOPSIS method, the modified TOPSIS approach was tested for this purpose.

Finally, the step of choosing different sorting methods, which is described as the fourth weakness, was tested on the VIKOR method. Again, first of all, the classical traditional VIKOR method was applied, then the value, which was considered as "0.5" in the traditional VIKOR method, was taken as "0.6" in the modified VIKOR approach, and differences were tried to be observed.

It is important to note that each of the flaws in the book's listed MCDM methods can also be applied to a preferred MCDM method. In some circumstances, the specified MCDM method can be used to address more than one of these flaws. Which weakness will be applied to which method has been chosen at random in order to better understand the topic, similar to the MCDM techniques recommended in the book. The application of the weaknesses to the aforementioned methods can be done in a variety of ways, including applying more than one weakness.

Finally, this study titled "Addressing the Weaknesses of Multi-Criteria Decision-Making Methods Using Python" is a very important and useful resource in terms of dealing with the "weaknesses" of MCDM methods, using both the traditional and modified methods while explaining the weaknesses, both theoretically and practically. Also, showing the applications with real data and using original data to analyze the economies of the world countries, and easily developing the results from today's popular coding languages by using Programs and the development of the results from the popular coding languages by the readers makes this study an important one. While the "weaknesses" mentioned in the book and the way the methods are applied are valid for all datasets, the developed Python codes require correction of variable names, etc. As a result of minor corrections, it is still valid for all data sets.

As a result, the study found that there were differences between the ranking of developed countries of the world and the rankings of IHDI obtained as a result of the traditional and modified ELECTRE, PROMEETHE, TOPSIS and VIKOR methods, which were used to highlight the weaknesses of the MCDM methods. The situation has once again drawn attention to the fact that HDI or IHDI values may change according to the approach, and hence the world's countries' development rankings may also change. The approaches discussed in the book can be handled in different ways such as fuzzy MCDM and artificial intelligence.

References

Anand, S., & Sen, A. (2010). The Income Component of the Human Development Index. *Journal of Human Development, 1*(1), pp. 83–106. https://doi.org/10.1080/14649880050008782

Anandan, V., & Uthra, G. (2017). Extension of TOPSIS Using L_1 Family of Distance. *Advances in Fuzzy Mathematics, 12*(4), pp. 897–908. https://www.ripublication.com/afm17/afmv12n4_11.pdf

Arend, R. J. (2020). Strategic Decision-Making Under Ambiguity: A New Problem Space and a Proposed Optimization Approach. *Business Research, 13*(3), pp. 1231–1251. https://doi.org/10.1007/s40685-020-00129-7

Atkinson, A. B. (1970). On the Measurement of Inequality. *Journal of Economic Theory, 2*(3), pp. 244–263. https://doi.org/10.1016/0022-0531(70)90039-6

Badings, T., Sim~ao, T. D., Suilen, M., & Jansen, N. (2023, March). Decision-Making Under Uncertainty: Beyond Probabilities. *International Journal on Software Tools for Technology Transfer*, pp. 1–18. https://doi.org/10.48550/arXiv.2303.05848

Ballestero, E. (2002). Strict Uncertainty: A Criterion for Moderately Pessimistic Decision Makers. *Decision Sciences, 33*(1), pp. 87–107. https://doi.org/10.1111/j.1540-5915.2002.tb01637.x

Basílio, M. P., Pereira, V., Costa, H. G., Santos, M., & Ghosh, A. (2022). A Systematic Review of the Applications of Multi-Criteria Decision Aid Methods (1977–2022). *Electronics, 11*(11), 1720. https://doi.org/10.3390/electronics11111720

Behzadian, M., Kazemzadeh, R., Albadvi, A., & Aghdasi, M. (2010). PROMETHEE: A Comprehensive Literature Review on Methodologies and Applications. *European Journal of Operational Research, 200*, pp. 198–215. https://doi.org/10.1016/j.ejor.2009.01.021

Belton, V., & Theodor, J. (2002). *Multiple Criteria Decision Analysis: An Integrated Approach*. Kluwer Academic Publishers. https://doi.org/10.1007/978-1-4615-1495-4

Bera, M. B., Mahapatra, B. S., Mondal, M. K., Acharjya, P. P., & Koley, S. (2023). A Comprehensive Review on Multicriteria Decision Making

Concepts and Their Applications. *Research Highlights in Science and Technology, 1*, pp. 103–114. https://doi.org/10.9734/bpi/rhst/v1/19058D

Brândaş, C. (2007). *Contributions to Conception, Design and Development of Decision Support Systems*. Cluj-Napoca: Babeş-Bolyai University.

Brans, J. P. (1982). Elaboration Dinstruments Daide a la Decision. In R. Nadeau, & M. Landry (Eds.), *Laide a la Decision: Nature, Instruments et Perspectives Davenir* (pp. 183–214). Canada: de Universite Laval.

Brans, J. P., & Mareschal, B. (1992). Promethee V: MCDM Problems With Segmentation Constraints. *INFOR: Information Systems and Operational Research, 30*(2). https://doi.org/10.1080/03155986.1992.11732186

Brans, J.-P., & Mareschal, B. (1995). The PROMETHEE VI Procedure: How to Differentiate Hard from Soft Multicriteria Problems. *Journal of Decision Systems, 4*(3). https://doi.org/10.1080/12460125.1995.10511652

Brans, J.-P., & Mareschal, B. (2005). Promethee Methods. In: Multiple Criteria Decision Analysis: State of the Art Surveys. In *International Series in Operations Research & Management Science*, vol 78. New York, NY: Springer. https://doi.org/10.1007/0-387-23081-5_5

Chatterjee, P. (2013). *Applications of Preference Ranking Based Methods for Decision Making in Manufacturing Environment*. Jadavpur University Department of Production Engineering. Retrieved from http://hdl.handle.net/10603/175990

Cornescu, V., Marinescu, P., Curteanu, D., & Toma, S. (1999). *Management: de la teorie la practica*. Editura Actarni.

Couger, J. (1996). Creativity/Innovation in Information Systems Organizations. *Proceedings of HICSS-29: 29th Hawaii International Conference on System Sciences*. Wailea, HI, USA: IEEE.

Couger, J. D. (1995). *Creative Problem Solving and Opportunity Finding*. Boyd & Fraser Pub Co.

Dearden, J. (1983, Fall). Will the Computer Change the Job of Top Management? *Sloan Management Review*, p. 57.

Delen, D. (2020). *Prescriptive Analytics: The Final Frontier for Evidence-Based Management and Optimal Decision Making*. USA: Pearson.

Deng, H. (2007). A Similarity-Based Approach to Ranking Multicriteria Alternatives. In D. Huang, L. Heutte, & M. Loog (Eds.), *Advanced Intelligent Computing Theories and Applications. With Aspects of Artificial Intelligence* (pp. 253–262). Berlin, Heidelberg: Springer. https://doi.org/10.1007/978-3-540-74205-0_28

Dyson, B. J. (2021). Variability in Competitive Decision-Making Speed and Quality Against Exploiting and Exploitative Opponents. *Scientific Reports, 11*(1), pp. 2859. https://doi.org/10.1038/s41598-021-82269-2

Engineer, M., King, I., & Roy, N. (2008). The Human Development Index as a Criterion for Optimal Planning. *Indian Growth and Development Review, 1*(2), pp. 172–192. https://doi.org/10.1108/1753825081 0903774

French, S. (1988). *Decision Theory: An Introduction to the Mathematics of Rationality*. New York: John Wiley & Sons.

Foster, J., Lopez-Calva, L., & Szekely, M. (2005). Measuring the Distribution of Human Development: Methodology and an Application to Mexico. *Journal of Human Development and Capabilities, 6*(1), pp. 5–25. https://doi.org/10.1080/14649880520003422220

Gorry, G. A., & Morton, M. S. (1971). *A Framework for Management Information Systems*. Cambridge, M.I.T.

Hammond, J. S., Keeney, R. L., & Raiffa, H. (1999). *Smart Choices: A Practical Guide to Making Better Decisions*. Boston: Harvard Business School Press.

Harttgen, K., & Vollmer, S. (2013). Using an Asset Index to Simulate Household Income. *Economics Letters, 121*(2), pp. 257–262. https://doi.org/10.1016/j.econlet.2013.08.014

Hassan, S. A., Tan, S. C., & Yusof, K. M. (2016). MCDM for Engineering Education: Literature Review and Research Issues. *World Engineering Education Forum & Global Engineering Deans Council, 627*, pp. 204–214. Springer. https://doi.org/10.1007/978-3-319-60937-9_16

HDI. (2022). *Human Development Index Technical Notes*. UNDP. Retrieved from https://hdr.undp.org/sites/default/files/2021-22_HDR/hdr2021-22_technical_notes.pdf

HDI. (2023). *HDI Dimensions and Indicators*. undp.org: Retrieved from https://hdr.undp.org/data-center/human-development-index#/indic ies/HDI

Hoven, J. V. (1996, March/April). Executive Support Systems & Decision Making. *Journal of Systems Management, 47*(2), pp. 48–55. https://www.proquest.com/scholarly-journals/executive-support-systems-amp-decision-making/docview/199818627/se-2

Hurwicz, L. (1951). Optimality Criteria for Decision Making under Ignorance. *Cowles Commission Discussion Paper, Statistics, 370,* pp. 1–11.

Hwang, C.-L., & Masud, A. S. (1979). *Multiple Objective Decision Making — Methods and Applications A State-of-the-Art Survey.* Berlin, Heidelberg: Springer-Verlag.

Hwang, C.-L., & Yoon, K. (1981). *Multiple Attribute Decision Making Methods and Applications A State-of-the-Art Survey* (1 b.). Berlin, Heidelberg: Springer. https://doi.org/10.1007/978-3-642-48318-9

IHDI. (2023). *Inequality-Adjusted Human Development Index (IHDI).* Retrieved from https://hdr.undp.org/inequality-adjusted-human-deve lopment-index#/indicies/IHDI

Insua, D. R. (1992). On the Foundations of Decision Making under Partial Information. *Theory and Decision, 33,* pp. 83–100. https://doi.org/ 10.1007/BF00133984

Jalal-Karim, A. (2013). Evaluating the Impact of Information Security on Enhancing the Business Decision-Making Process. *World Journal of Entrepreneurship, Management and Sustainable Development, 9*(1), pp. 55–64. https://doi.org/10.1108/20425961311315719

Jett, Q. R., & George, J. M. (2005). Emergent Strategies and Their Consequences: A Process Study of Competition and Complex Decision Making. In G. Szulanski, J. Porac, & Y. Doz (Eds.), (pp. 387–411). Emerald Group Publishing Limited. https://doi.org/10.1016/ S0742-3322(05)22013-2

Kahneman, D., & Deaton, A. (2010). High Income Improves Evaluation of Life But Not Emotional Well-Being. *Psychological and Cognitive Sciences, 107*(38), pp. 16489–16493. https://doi.org/10.1073/pnas.101 1492107

Kepner, C. H., & Tregoe, B. B. (1965). *The Rational Manager: A Systematic Approach to Problem Solving and Decision-Making* (First Edition b.). McGraw-Hill Book Company.

Kovacevic, M. S. (2010/33). *Review of HDI Critiques and Potential Improvements Human Development Research Paper.* UNDP. https:// hdr.undp.org/content/review-hdi-critiques-and-potential-improvements

Krstić, M., Agnusdei, G. P., Miglietta, P. P., Tadić, S., & Roso, V. (2022). Applicability of Industry 4.0 Technologies in the Reverse Logistics: A

Circular Economy Approach Based on Comprehensive Distance Based Ranking (COBRA) Method. *Sustainability, 14*(9), 5632, https://doi.org/10.3390/su14095632

Laplace, M. d. (1985). *Essai philosophique sur les probabilites*. Paris (A philosophical essay on probabilities).

Li, H.-F., & Wang, J.-J. (2007). An Improved Ranking Method for ELECTRE III. In *2007 International Conference on Wireless Communications, Networking and Mobile Computing* (s. 6659–6662). Shanghai, China: IEEE. https://doi.org/10.1109/WICOM.2007.1634

Luce, R. D., & Raiffa, H. (1957). *Games and Decisions: Introduction and Critical Survey*. Wiley.

Macharis, C., Brans, J.-P., & Mareschal, B. (1998). The GDSS Promethee Procedure. *Journal of Decision Systems, 7*(4), pp. 283–307.

Mastrodomenico, R. (2022). *The Python Book*. Wiley.

McKinney, W. (2017). *Python for Data Analysis: Data Wrangling with Pandas, NumPy, and IPython*. O'Reilly UK Ltd.

Ming, T., & Huchang, L. (2021). From Conventional Group Decision Making to Large-scale Group Decision Making: What Are the Challenges and How to Meet Them in Big Data Era? A State-of-the-Art Survey. *Omega, 100*. https://doi.org/10.1016/j.omega.2019.102141.

Negulescu, O.-H. (2014). Using A Decision-Making Process Model. *Review of General Management, 19*(1), pp. 111–123.

Nickel. (2022). An Overview of Decision-Making Models. Retrieved from An Overview of Decision-Making Models - ToughNickel on 05.12.2023

Nobrega, R., O'Hara, C., Sadasivuni, R., & Dumas, J. (2009). Bridging Decision-Making Process and Environmental Needs in Corridor Planning. *Management of Environmental Quality, 20*(6), pp. 622–637. https://doi.org/10.1108/14777830910990744

Nooraie, M. (2008). Decision Magnitude of Impact and Strategic Decision-Making Process Output. *Management Decision, 46*(4), pp. 640–655. https://doi.org/10.1108/00251740810865102

Omrani, H., Alizadeh, A., & Amini, M. (2020). A New Approach Based on BWM and MULTIMOORA Methods for Calculating Semi-Human Development Index: An Application for Provinces of Iran. *Socio-Economic Planning Sciences, 70*, pp. 1–11. https://doi.org/10.1016/j.seps.2019.02.004.

Opricovic, S. (1998). Multicriteria Optimization of Civil Engineering Systems. *Faculty of Civil Engineering, Belgrade, 2*(1), pp. 5–21.

Opricovic, S., & Tzeng, G.-H. (2007). Extended VIKOR Method in Comparison with Outranking Methods. *European Journal of Operational Research, 178*(2), pp. 514–529. https://doi.org/10.1016/j.ejor.2006.01.020

Pažek, K. & Rozman, Č. (2009). Decision Making under Conditions of Uncertainty in Agriculture: A Case Study of Oil Crops. *Agriculture, 15*(1), pp. 45–50.

Peters, J. (1999). The Managerial Decision-Making Process. *Management Decision, 37*(5), pp. 57–58. https://doi.org/10.1108/md.1999.37.5.57.1

Pokras, S. (1989). *Systematic Problem-Solving and Decision-Making.* Crisp Pub Inc.

Pounds, W. F. (1969, Fall). The Process of Problem Finding. *Industrial Management Review (pre–1986)*, pp. 1–19.

Rezaei, J. (2015). Best-Worst Multi-Criteria Decision-Making Method. *Omega, 53*, pp. 49–57. https://doi.org/10.1016/j.omega.2014.11.009

Rezaei, J. (2016). Best-Worst Multi-Criteria Decision-Making Method: Some Properties and a Linear Model. *Omega, 64*, pp. 126–130. https://doi.org/10.1016/j.omega.2015.12.001

Roy, B. (1978). ELECTRE III: Algorithme de Classement Basé sur une Représentation Floue des Préférences en Présence de Critères Multiples. *Cahiers du CERO, 20*(1), pp. 3–24.

Roy, B., & Bertier, P. (1973). La méthode electre II: une application au media-planning; the electre II method, an application to media planning. In *Or; proceedings of the IFORS International Conference on Operational Research*, (pp. 291–302). Amsterdam.

Roy, B., & Hugonnard, J. (1982). Ranking of Suburban Line Extension Projects on the Paris Metro System by a Multicriteria Method. *Transportation Research Part A: General, 16*(4), pp. 301–312.

Roy, B., & Skalka, J. (1984). ELECTRE IS: Aspects Méthodologiques et Guide D'utilisation. *Document du Lamsade, 30.*

Saaty, T. L. (2008). Decision Making with the Analytic Hierarchy Process. *International Journal of Services Sciences, 1*(1), pp. 83–98. https://doi.org/10.1504/IJSSCI.2008.017590

Sabaei, D., Erkoyuncu, J., & Roy, R. (2015). *A Review of Multi-Criteria Decision Making Methods for Enhanced Maintenance Delivery.* https://doi.org/10.1016/j.procir.2015.08.086.

Safari, H., & Ebrahimi, E. (2014). Using Modified Similarity Multiple Criteria Decision Making Technique to Rank Countries in Terms of Human Development Index. *Journal of Industrial Engineering and Management (JIEM)*, 7(1), pp. 254–275. http://dx.doi.org/10.3926/jiem.837

Savage, L. J. (1951). The Theory of Statistical Decision. *Journal of the American Statistical Association*, 46(253), pp. 55–67.

Sharda, R., Delen, D., & Turban, E. (2013). *Business Intelligence and Analytics: Systems for Decision Support.* Pearson.

Simon, H. A. (1977). *The New Science of Management Decision.* New Jersey: Prentice-Hall.

Singh, M., Baranwal, G., & Tripathi, A. K. (2023). Decentralized Group Decision Making Using Blockchain. *The Journal of Supercomputing, 79*, pp. 20141–20178. https://doi.org/10.1007/s11227-023-05426-6

Śleszyński, J. (2016). Human Development Index Revisited. *Research Papers of Wrocław University of Economics*, pp. 40–54. http://doi.org/10.15611/pn.2016.435.02

Taha, H. A. (2007). *Operations Research an Introduction* (8th ed.). Pearson Prentice Hall.

Taşabat, S. E. (2019). A Novel Multicriteria Decision-Making Method Based on Distance, Similarity, and Correlation: DSC TOPSIS. *Mathematical Problems in Engineering*, 20. https://doi.org/10.1155/2019/9125754

Taşabat, S. E., & Başer, B. (2017). The Analysis of Human Development Levels Via Multi-Criteria Decision Making Methods with Different Weighting Techniques: The Case of European Union Members, Candidates and Potential Candidates. *International Journal of Recent Advances in Multidisciplinary Research*, 4(11), pp. 3022–3029.

Taşabat, S. E., & Özkan, T. K. (2020). TOPSIS vs. VIKOR: A Case Study for Determining Development Level of Countries. In A. Behl (Ed.), *Multi-Criteria Decision Analysis in Management* (pp. 225–250). http://doi.org/10.4018/978-1-7998-2216-5.ch010

Triantaphyllou, E. (2000). *Multi-criteria Decision Making Methods: A Comparative Study.* Boston, MA: Springer. https://doi.org/10.1007/978-1-4757-3157-6_2

Turskis, Z., & Zavadskas, E. K. (2011). Multiple Criteria Decision Making (MCDM) Methods in Economics: An Overview. *Technological and Economic Development of Economy,* pp. 397–427. https://doi.org/10.3846/20294913.2011.593291

UNDP. (2023). *Human Development Reports.* Retrieved from https://hdr.undp.org/about-hdro

Verboncu, I. (2011). Managerial Methodologization and Its Impact on the Managerial Efficiency and Effectiveness. *Review of General Management, 13*(1), pp. 34–43.

Wald, A. (1949, June). Statistical Decision Functions. *The Annals of Mathematical Statistics, 20*(2), pp. 165–205. Retrieved from https://www.jstor.org/stable/2236853

Weller, S. C., & Romney, A. K. (1990). *Metric Scaling: Correspondence Analysis.* Newbury Park: Sage Publications.

Wen, M., & Iwamura, K. (2008). Fuzzy Facility Location-Allocation Problem under the Hurwicz Criterion. *European Journal of Operational Research, 184*(2), pp. 627–635. https://doi.org/10.1016/j.ejor.2006.11.029

Wildman, J. L., & Salas, E. (2009). Making It Practical: Simulation, Naturalistic Decision Making, and Complexity in Team Performance. In F. J. Yammarino, & F. Dansereau (Dü) (Eds.), *Multi-Level Issues in Organizational Behavior and Leadership* (pp. 301–309). Publisher: Emerald Group Publishing Limited. https://doi.org/10.1108/S1475-9144(2009)0000008013

Xiaomei, M., Ming, T., Huchang, L., Wenjing, S., & Lev, B. (2019). The State-of-the-Art Survey on Integrations and Applications of the Best Worst Method in Decision Making: Why, What, What for and What's Next? *Omega, 87,* pp. 205–225. https://doi.org/10.1016/j.omega.2019.01.009

Yu, W. (1992). *ELECTRE Tri: Aspects methodologiques et manual d'utilisation.* Document de LAMSADE. Paris: Universite Paris-Dauphine.

ZeinEldin, R. A., & Khater, E. (2013). A Multicriteria Approach for Developing New Human Development Index. *International Journal of Contemporary Mathematical Sciences, 1,* pp. 31–40. http://dx.doi.org/10.12988/ijcms.2013.13003

Appendix Comparison of Traditional and Modified Methods Results

rank	Modified ELECTRE III	Traditional ELECTRE III	Modified TOPSIS	Traditional TOPSIS	Traditional PROMETHEE	Modified PROMETHEE	Traditional VIKOR	Modified VIKOR
1	Iceland	Iceland	Norway	Iceland	Iceland	Iceland	Norway	Norway
2	Norway	Norway	Iceland	Norway	Norway	Norway	Iceland	Iceland
3	Switzerland	Switzerland	Finland	Denmark	Denmark	Ireland	Denmark	Denmark
4	Finland	Finland	Switzerland	Switzerland	Switzerland	Switzerland	Slovenia	Slovenia
5	Sweden	Sweden	Sweden	Finland	Ireland	Denmark	Ireland	Finland
6	Australia	Australia	Denmark	Sweden	Finland	Sweden	Austria	New Zealand
7	Denmark	Denmark	Slovenia	Germany	Sweden	Finland	Switzerland	Switzerland
8	Germany	Germany Netherlands	Netherlands	Ireland	Germany	Belgium	Netherlands	Sweden
9	Netherlands	Ireland	Germany	Netherlands	Netherlands	Australia	Finland	Ireland
10	Ireland	Slovenia New Zealand Canada	Ireland	Slovenia	Belgium	Netherlands	Australia	Australia
11	New Zealand	Belgium	Belgium	Belgium	Australia	Germany	Germany	Germany
12	Slovenia Canada	United Kingdom	Czechia	Australia	Slovenia	Luxembourg	United Kingdom	United Kingdom
13	Belgium	Malta	Australia	New Zealand	New Zealand	Slovenia	Belgium	Belgium
14	United Kingdom	Austria Japan	New Zealand	Canada	Canada	Japan	Luxembourg	Luxembourg
15	Malta	Czechia	Canada	Austria	Luxembourg	Malta	Sweden	Netherlands
16	Austria Japan	Estonia	Austria	Czechia	Japan	Korea (Republic of)	Canada	Austria

rank	Modified ELECTRE III	Traditional ELECTRE III	Modified TOPSIS	Traditional TOPSIS	Traditional PROMETHEE	Modified PROMETHEE	Traditional VIKOR	Modified VIKOR
17	Czechia	Luxembourg Korea (Republic of)	Malta	United Kingdom	Austria	Hong Kong, China (SAR)	Malta	Malta
18	Estonia	United States	Estonia	Luxembourg	Malta	Austria	New Zealand	Canada
19	Luxembourg	Hong Kong, China (SAR)	United Kingdom	Malta	United Kingdom	New Zealand	Korea (Republic of)	Korea (Republic of)
20	Korea (Republic of)	Singapore	Poland	Japan	Czechia	Canada	Czechia	Japan
21	United States	Israel	Japan	Korea (Republic of)	Korea (Republic of)	France	Hungary	Croatia
22	Hong Kong, China (SAR)	Poland	United States	Estonia	Hong Kong, China (SAR)	Singapore	Poland	Cyprus
23	Singapore Israel	France	Luxembourg	United States	France	Cyprus	United States	United States
24	Poland	Cyprus	Korea (Republic of)	France	Singapore	United Kingdom	Estonia	Estonia
25	France	Greece	Slovakia	Hong Kong, China (SAR)	Estonia	Czechia	Hong Kong, China (SAR)	Hong Kong, China (SAR)
26	Cyprus	Croatia	Lithuania	Poland	Cyprus	Israel	Japan	Czechia
27	Greece	Italy	Latvia	Cyprus	Israel	Spain	France	France
28	Croatia	Slovakia Lithuania	Croatia	Singapore	United States	Italy	Belarus	Portugal
29	Italy	Latvia	Hungary	Israel	Poland	Estonia	Montenegro	Montenegro
30	Slovakia Lithuania	Montenegro	Hong Kong, China (SAR)	Slovakia	Italy	Portugal	Israel	Israel
31	Latvia Montenegro	Hungary	Cyprus	Lithuania	Spain	Greece	Singapore	Poland

ppendix 147

rank	Modified ELECTRE III	Traditional ELECTRE III	Modified TOPSIS	Traditional TOPSIS	Traditional PROMETHEE	Modified PROMETHEE	Traditional VIKOR	Modified VIKOR
32	Hungary	Spain	France	Croatia	Slovakia	Poland	Cyprus	Singapore
33	Spain	Portugal	Belarus	Latvia	Lithuania	United States	Lithuania	Lithuania
34	Portugal Belarus	Belarus	Singapore	Hungary	Greece	Croatia	Greece	Hungary
35	Romania	Romania	Israel	Greece	Croatia	Slovakia	Portugal	Belarus
36	Serbia	Serbia	Greece	Italy	Latvia	Hungary	Croatia	Latvia
37	Chile	Chile	Russian Federation	Spain	Hungary	Lithuania	Italy	Italy
38	Türkiye	Türkiye	Kazakhstan	Portugal	Portugal	Latvia	Spain	Spain
39	Albania	Albania	Italy	Belarus	Kazakhstan	Montenegro	Slovakia	Slovakia
40	Bulgaria	Bulgaria	Ukraine	Kazakhstan	Belarus	Chile	Latvia	Greece
41	Uruguay	Uruguay	Romania	Montenegro	Russian Federation	Belarus	Russian Federation	Russian Federation
42	Ukraine	Ukraine	Montenegro	Russian Federation	Montenegro	Kazakhstan	Ukraine	Ukraine
43	Oman	Oman Iran (Islamic Republic of)	Spain	Romania	Argentina	Romania	Romania	Romania
44	Iran (Islamic Republic of)	Argentina North Macedonia	Moldova (Republic of)	Ukraine	Chile	Russian Federation	Kazakhstan	Kazakhstan
45	Argentina North Macedonia	Russian Federation	Portugal	Argentina	Romania	Türkiye	Chile	Chile
46	Russian Federation	Georgia Armenia	Serbia	Chile	Georgia	Thailand	Türkiye	Türkiye
47	Georgia Armenia	Thailand	Oman	Serbia	Ukraine	Serbia	Oman	Oman

rank	Modified ELECTRE III	Traditional ELECTRE III	Modified TOPSIS	Traditional TOPSIS	Traditional PROMETHEE	Modified PROMETHEE	Traditional VIKOR	Modified VIKOR
48	Thailand	Bosnia and Herzegovina	Bulgaria	Türkiye	Moldova (Republic of)	Albania	Armenia	Armenia
49	Bosnia and Herzegovina	Sri Lanka	Argentina	Oman	Serbia	Argentina	Argentina	Argentina
50	Sri Lanka	Kazakhstan	Azerbaijan	Moldova (Republic of)	Türkiye	Uruguay	Serbia	Serbia
51	Kazakhstan	Costa Rica Seychelles	Albania	Uruguay	Uruguay	Ukraine	Georgia	Albania
52	Costa Rica Seychelles	Panama	Türkiye	Albania	Oman	China	Uruguay	Uruguay
53	Panama	Mauritius	Georgia	Georgia	Albania	Maldives	Bulgaria	Bulgaria
54	Mauritius	Tonga	Uruguay	Bulgaria	Bulgaria	Sri Lanka	Costa Rica	Sri Lanka
55	Tonga Mongolia	Mongolia	Armenia	Armenia	Tonga	Costa Rica	Moldova (Republic of)	Moldova (Republic of)
56	Peru	Peru	Chile	Iran (Islamic Republic of)	Iran (Islamic Republic of)	Oman	Barbados	Costa Rica
57	Moldova (Republic of) China	Moldova (Republic of) China	Iran (Islamic Republic of)	Azerbaijan	Armenia	Bosnia and Herzegovina	North Macedonia	Iran (Islamic Republic of)
58	Azerbaijan Mexico	Azerbaijan Mexico	North Macedonia	North Macedonia	Azerbaijan	Moldova (Republic of)	Mauritius	Mauritius
59	Barbados Jordan	Barbados	Seychelles	Thailand	Barbados	Georgia	Thailand	Thailand
60	Algeria	Jordan	Tonga	Bosnia and Herzegovina	Thailand	North Macedonia	Albania	Georgia

rank	Modified ELECTRE III	Traditional ELECTRE III	Modified TOPSIS	Traditional TOPSIS	Traditional PROMETHEE	Modified PROMETHEE	Traditional VIKOR	Modified VIKOR
61	Dominican Republic Viet Nam	Algeria	Turkmenistan	Sri Lanka	Sri Lanka	Bulgaria	Sri Lanka	Bosnia and Herzegovina
62	Tunisia	Dominican Republic	Mauritius	Mauritius	Costa Rica	Barbados	Iran (Islamic Republic of)	North Macedonia
63	Kyrgyzstan Ecuador	Viet Nam	Mongolia	Seychelles	North Macedonia	Iran (Islamic Republic of)	China	Barbados
64	Paraguay	Tunisia	Sri Lanka	Tonga	Bosnia and Herzegovina	Armenia	Azerbaijan	Azerbaijan
65	Saint Lucia	Kyrgyzstan Ecuador	Bosnia and Herzegovina	Costa Rica	Seychelles	Azerbaijan	Mongolia	Mongolia
66	Turkmenistan	Paraguay Saint Lucia	Thailand	Barbados	Mauritius	Mauritius	Bosnia and Herzegovina	Tonga
67	Tajikistan El Salvador	Turkmenistan	Kyrgyzstan	China	Kyrgyzstan	Tonga	Dominican Republic	Jordan
68	Colombia Indonesia	Tajikistan El Salvador	Costa Rica	Panama	China	Panama	Seychelles	China
69	Samoa Maldives	Colombia	Peru	Mongolia	Turkmenistan	Seychelles	Jordan	Dominican Republic
70	Philippines	Indonesia	Dominican Republic	Peru	Panama	Peru	Tonga	Seychelles
71	Jamaica Brazil	Samoa Maldives Guyana	Barbados	Turkmenistan	Peru	Mongolia	Ecuador	Ecuador
72	Iraq	Philippines	Mexico	Mexico	Mongolia	Jordan	Samoa	Samoa
73	Venezuela (Bolivarian Republic of)	Jamaica Brazil	Panama	Kyrgyzstan	Samoa	Kyrgyzstan	Panama	Panama

rank	Modified ELECTRE III	Traditional ELECTRE III	Modified TOPSIS	Traditional TOPSIS	Traditional PROMETHEE	Modified PROMETHEE	Traditional VIKOR	Modified VIKOR
74	Palestine, State of Tuvalu	Iraq	China	Dominican Republic	Mexico	Algeria	Peru	Peru
75	Gabon	Venezuela (Bolivarian Republic of) Palestine, State of	Guyana	Jordan	Tajikistan	Mexico	Turkmenistan	Turkmenistan
76	Egypt	Tuvalu	Tajikistan	Samoa	Dominican Republic	Ecuador	Egypt	El Salvador
77	Bolivia (Plurinational State of)	Gabon	Samoa	Ecuador	Venezuela (Bolivarian Republic of)	Dominican Republic	Venezuela (Bolivarian Republic of)	Venezuela (Bolivarian Republic of)
78	Nicaragua Kiribati	Egypt	Venezuela (Bolivarian Republic of)	Algeria	Ecuador	Samoa	Mexico	Mexico
79	Bangladesh	Bolivia (Plurinational State of)	Bolivia (Plurinational State of)	Viet Nam	Jamaica	Viet Nam	Kyrgyzstan	Kyrgyzstan
80	Morocco Sao Tome and Principe	Nicaragua Kiribati	Indonesia	Tajikistan	Colombia	Tunisia	Algeria	Tajikistan
81	India	Bangladesh	Jordan	Maldives	Jordan	Colombia	Viet Nam	Viet Nam
82	Suriname	Morocco	Jamaica	Guyana	Palestine, State of	Tajikistan	Jamaica	Guyana
83	Belize Cambodia	Sao Tome and Principe	Ecuador	Colombia	Philippines	Turkmenistan	Guyana	Jamaica
84	Honduras	India	Philippines	Venezuela (Bolivarian Republic of)	Brazil	Venezuela (Bolivarian Republic of)	Indonesia	Indonesia

rank	Modified ELECTRE III	Traditional ELECTRE III	Modified TOPSIS	Traditional TOPSIS	Traditional PROMETHEE	Modified PROMETHEE	Traditional VIKOR	Modified VIKOR
85	Guatemala Lao People's Democratic Republic	Belize Suriname	Viet Nam	Jamaica	Paraguay	Jamaica	Maldives	Algeria
86	Ghana Nepal	Cambodia	Paraguay	Tunisia	Viet Nam	Paraguay	Tunisia	Tunisia
87	Bhutan	Honduras	Gabon	Indonesia	Guyana	Palestine, State of	Colombia	Colombia
88	Tanzania (United Republic of)	Guatemala Lao People's Democratic Republic	Colombia	Palestine, State of	Indonesia	Indonesia	Paraguay	Paraguay
89	Congo Kenya	Ghana	Algeria	Paraguay	Maldives	Brazil	Tajikistan	Maldives
90	Papua New Guinea	Nepal Timor-Leste	Palestine, State of	Brazil	Bolivia (Plurinational State of)	Philippines	Nicaragua	Suriname
91	South Africa Zimbabwe	Bhutan	Maldives	Philippines	Algeria	Saint Lucia	Bolivia (Plurinational State of)	Bolivia (Plurinational State of)
92	Angola	Tanzania (United Republic of)	Tuvalu	Gabon	Tunisia	Iraq	Palestine, State of	Palestine, State of
93	Eswatini (Kingdom of)	Congo Kenya	Brazil	Saint Lucia	Tuvalu	Guyana	Suriname	Nicaragua
94	Rwanda	Papua New Guinea	Tunisia	Iraq	Gabon	El Salvador	Kiribati	Kiribati
95	Uganda	South Africa	Iraq	Bolivia (Plurinational State of)	Saint Lucia	Egypt	Philippines	Philippines
96	Mauritania	Zimbabwe	Kiribati	El Salvador	Suriname	Morocco	Belize	Egypt

rank	Modified ELECTRE III	Traditional ELECTRE III	Modified TOPSIS	Traditional TOPSIS	Traditional PROMETHEE	Modified PROMETHEE	Traditional VIKOR	Modified VIKOR
97	Pakistan	Angola	Saint Lucia	Suriname	Belize	Nicaragua	Tuvalu	Tuvalu
98	Namibia Cameroon	Eswatini (Kingdom of)	South Africa	Belize	El Salvador	Belize	Brazil	Brazil
99	Togo	Rwanda Uganda	Suriname	Tuvalu	Iraq	Bangladesh	Gabon	Gabon
100	Ethiopia Côte d'Ivoire	Mauritania	Belize	Egypt	Kiribati	Suriname	Iraq	Iraq
101	Madagascar Gambia	Pakistan	Nicaragua	Nicaragua	Egypt	Tuvalu	India	Cambodia
102	Zambia Malawi	Namibia	El Salvador	Morocco	Nicaragua	Gabon	Saint Lucia	Saint Lucia
103	Benin	Cameroon	Zimbabwe	Kiribati	Sao Tome and Principe	Bolivia (Plurinational State of)	El Salvador	Belize
104	Senegal Liberia	Togo	Egypt	Bangladesh	Bangladesh	Sao Tome and Principe	Zimbabwe	Lao People's Democratic Republic
105	Lesotho Sudan	Ethiopia Côte d'Ivoire	Morocco	South Africa	South Africa	Bhutan	Bangladesh	Morocco
106	Comoros	Madagascar	Honduras	Sao Tome and Principe	Morocco	Cambodia	Honduras	Bangladesh
107	Congo (Democratic Republic of the)	Gambia	Sao Tome and Principe	Bhutan	Honduras	Kiribati	Sao Tome and Principe	Sao Tome and Principe
108	Sierra Leone Guinea-Bissau	Zambia	Bangladesh	India	India	Guatemala	South Africa	India
109	Yemen	Malawi	Bhutan	Honduras	Cambodia	India	Guatemala	Guatemala
110	Burkina Faso	Senegal	India	Cambodia	Bhutan	Honduras	Morocco	Honduras

rank	Modified ELECTRE III	Traditional ELECTRE III	Modified TOPSIS	Traditional TOPSIS	Traditional PROMETHEE	Modified PROMETHEE	Traditional VIKOR	Modified VIKOR
111	Mozambique	Benin Liberia	Lao People's Democratic Republic	Guatemala	Ghana	Nepal	Nepal	Zimbabwe
112	Guinea	Lesotho Sudan Haiti	Ghana	Lao People's Democratic Republic	Guatemala	Lao People's Democratic Republic	Lao People's Democratic Republic	Ghana
113	Niger	Comoros	Cambodia	Zimbabwe	Zimbabwe	Timor-Leste	Cambodia	South Africa
114	Nigeria Mali	Congo (Democratic Republic of the)	Eswatini (Kingdom of)	Ghana	Lao People's Democratic Republic	Ghana	Bhutan	Bhutan
115	Chad South Sudan Central African Republic	Sierra Leone Guinea-Bissau Burundi	Timor-Leste	Nepal	Nepal	South Africa	Kenya	Kenya
116		Yemen	Guatemala	Timor-Leste	Timor-Leste	Tanzania (United Republic of)	Congo	Congo
117		Burkina Faso Mozambique	Nepal	Eswatini (Kingdom of)	Congo	Papua New Guinea	Ghana	Nepal
118		Nigeria	Congo	Congo	Kenya	Congo	Timor-Leste	Timor-Leste
119		Guinea	Lesotho	Kenya	Eswatini (Kingdom of)	Senegal	Rwanda	Angola
120		Mali	Mauritania	Tanzania (United Republic of)	Tanzania (United Republic of)	Rwanda	Pakistan	Mauritania
121		Niger	Angola	Angola	Namibia	Kenya	Namibia	Rwanda
122		Chad South Sudan Central African Republic	Pakistan	Mauritania	Angola	Pakistan	Mauritania	Zambia

rank	Modified ELECTRE III	Traditional ELECTRE III	Modified TOPSIS	Traditional TOPSIS	Traditional PROMETHEE	Modified PROMETHEE	Traditional VIKOR	Modified VIKOR
123			Kenya	Namibia	Papua New Guinea	Mauritania	Tanzania (United Republic of)	Tanzania (United Republic of)
124			Namibia	Pakistan	Rwanda	Zimbabwe	Uganda	Papua New Guinea
125			Zambia	Papua New Guinea	Zambia	Ethiopia	Eswatini (Kingdom of)	Eswatini (Kingdom of)
126			Nigeria	Rwanda	Mauritania	Uganda	Cameroon	Cameroon
127			Cameroon	Zambia	Cameroon	Angola	Angola	Namibia
128			Côte d'Ivoire	Cameroon	Uganda	Namibia	Lesotho	Togo
129			Rwanda	Uganda	Pakistan	Eswatini (Kingdom of)	Papua New Guinea	Uganda
130			Tanzania (United Republic of)	Senegal	Malawi	Malawi	Senegal	Senegal
131			Papua New Guinea	Lesotho	Togo	Sudan	Zambia	Pakistan
132			Ethiopia	Ethiopia	Senegal	Madagascar	Madagascar	Madagascar
133			Senegal	Côte d'Ivoire	Ethiopia	Gambia	Togo	Lesotho
134			Congo (Democratic Republic of the)	Malawi	Madagascar	Zambia	Comoros	Liberia
135			Uganda	Togo	Côte d'Ivoire	Cameroon	Malawi	Malawi
136			Malawi	Nigeria	Lesotho	Togo	Nigeria	Gambia

rank	Modified ELECTRE III	Traditional ELECTRE III	Modified TOPSIS	Traditional TOPSIS	Traditional PROMETHEE	Modified PROMETHEE	Traditional VIKOR	Modified VIKOR
137			Guinea	Madagascar	Gambia	Côte d'Ivoire	Sudan	Congo (Democratic Republic of the)
138			Gambia	Gambia	Sudan	Yemen	Ethiopia	Ethiopia
139			Madagascar	Sudan	Haiti	Haiti	Sierra Leone	Burkina Faso
140			Burkina Faso	Benin	Benin	Comoros	Congo (Democratic Republic of the)	Sudan
141			Benin	Congo (Democratic Republic of the)	Comoros	Benin	Gambia	Nigeria
142			Togo	Haiti	Nigeria	Liberia	Côte d'Ivoire	Côte d'Ivoire
143			Mali	Comoros	Congo (Democratic Republic of the)	Burkina Faso	Benin	Benin
144			Sudan	Guinea	Liberia	Burundi	Burkina Faso	Comoros
145			Sierra Leone	Burkina Faso	Yemen	Niger	Haiti	Sierra Leone
146			Comoros	Liberia	Burkina Faso	Congo (Democratic Republic of the)	Mozambique	Mozambique
147			Haiti	Mali	Guinea-Bissau	Guinea-Bissau	Liberia	Haiti
148			Yemen	Yemen	Sierra Leone	Guinea	Yemen	Yemen
149			Liberia	Sierra Leone	Guinea	Mali	Burundi	Guinea-Bissau
150			Burundi	Guinea-Bissau	Burundi	Sierra Leone	Guinea	Guinea

rank	Modified ELECTRE III	Traditional ELECTRE III	Modified TOPSIS	Traditional TOPSIS	Traditional PROMETHEE	Modified PROMETHEE	Traditional VIKOR	Modified VIKOR
151			Niger	Niger	Mozambique	Mozambique	Niger	Niger
152			Chad	Burundi	Mali	Lesotho	Guinea-Bissau	Burundi
153			Mozambique	Mozambique	Niger	Nigeria	Chad	Chad
154			Guinea-Bissau	Chad	Chad	Chad	Mali	Mali
155			Central African Republic	Central African Republic	Central African Republic	South Sudan	South Sudan	South Sudan
156			South Sudan	South Sudan	South Sudan	Central African Republic	Central African Republic	Central African Republic